The Irish Cookbook The Ultimate Guide To Irish Classic Recipes And Its History Food

Paul McGregor

Published by vincenzo nappi, 2021.

THE IRISH COOKBOOK THE ULTIMATE GUIDE TO IRISH CLASSIC RECIPES AND ITS HISTORY FOOD

First edition. September 9, 2021.

Copyright © 2021 Paul McGregor.

ISBN: 979-8215535905

Written by Paul McGregor.

Also by Paul McGregor

The Irish Cookbook The Ultimate Guide To Irish Classic Recipes
And Its History Food

THE IRISH COOKBOOK

The Ultimate Guide To Irish Classic Recipes And Its History Food

by

Paul McGregor

1

within this document, including, but not limited to, — errors, omissions, or inaccuracies.

INTRODUCTION

———

The classic dishes of rural Ireland, remain the country's mainstay. Boxty and bannocks, colcannon and champ are just a few of the traditional dishes that contribute to the rich variety of this country's cuisine. These recipes, together with such delights as drisheen and dankey stew, reflect the culinary ingenuity of the Irish people, and are fundamentals of the Irish country kitchen. Irish food remains basically simple. It consists of local ingredients used at their best so that fresh, wholesome and succulent food can still be enjoyed now as it was thousands of years ago.

It is through the homely recipes of traditional Ireland that the rich tapestry of Irish history can be traced. For many millennia, Ireland has been an agricultural country, and fields on the island today were cultivated in prehistoric times. 'Time is the best storyteller' is an early Irish saying that can be applied equally to the country's food. In this book we have combined snippets from Irish history with descriptions of various ingredients and typical traditional Irish recipes, demonstrating the link between the country's past and its present-day cuisine.

Using the Recipes

All the recipe ingredients are given in metric, imperial and American cup measures. Where the names are different, American terms are given in brackets. All spoon measurements are level. You should use accurate measuring spoons for best results, using a 5 ml spoon for 1 teaspoon and a 15 ml spoon for 1 tablespoon. Unless otherwise stated, the ingredients included in the recipes – such as vegetables or fruit – are medium size. All fresh ingredients should be washed and peeled where necessary. Medium-sized eggs are used in all cases, except where stated otherwise.

Eggs should always be eaten by the sell-by date and should never be used if the shells are already cracked. Pregnant women, the very young, the elderly and anyone with a specific medical condition should refer to approved guidelines before eating eggs and should particularly avoid raw or partially cooked eggs. Fresh herbs are preferable to dried varieties. Dried herbs can be substituted where fresh herbs are unavailable, but half the quantity indicated is sufficient. Fresh herbs can easily be grown at home and they do impart a unique flavour to some of the recipes. Can weights are approximate as they vary between brands. Canned beans and pulses can be used instead of dried. If you substitute canned for dried, the weight of the prepared ingredients will be about twice the weight of the dried ingredients. For example, if the recipe calls for 225 g/ 8 oz/ 1 1/3 cups dried pulses, substitute with a 425 g/ 15 oz/ large can. Note that dried kidney beans contain harmful toxins and should always be fast-boiled for around 20 minutes to destroy the toxins. Some of the recipes contain whole or chopped nuts or nut oil and are therefore not suitable for young children or those with any form of nut-related allergy.

Oven settings vary considerably between different types of cooker, so you should check and adjust the cooking temperatures to suit your own oven. Gas ovens, for example, are hotter towards the top of the oven, while if you are using a fan-assisted oven, you may need to reduce the oven temperature. Cooking times indicated in the recipes are approximate and are usually rounded up to the nearest five minutes. Fan ovens tend to cook faster than others so always refer to your handbook and adjust times to suit your own equipment.

Baking

From the grasses that grew wild in prehistoric times, a range of cereals developed – such as millet, sorghum, rice, maize, wheat, barley and oats – which came to be cultivated by early peoples. Our word 'cereal' comes from the Roman goddess of the harvest, Ceres, as it was the Romans who brought the use of grains to Britain and thence to Ireland, where many grew well in the temperate climate. Many different cereals are ground to produce flour for baking or cooking, but only wheat produces a flour with rising properties, due to its high gluten content – gluten being the sticky, nitrogenous part of the flour which absorbs water.

The more gluten in the flour, the better the rising qualities of the mix, so the strong, or brown, flours are the ones used in Irish yeast and bread baking. Softer flours, with a lower gluten content but a higher starch content, are reserved for making cakes and biscuits, as the starch ensures that the flour absorbs more fat, and a raising agent is added to the dough to compensate for the lower gluten.

All kinds of flour are used in the baking of Irish breads. If the whole of the wheat berry is ground, the flour is wholemeal or wholewheat, which is high in dietary fibre as it contains the bran, or outer husk. Often, however, the bran is removed after grinding. Some Irish breads used to use wheatmeal flour, which is flour with about ten per cent of the bran removed, although this type of flour is no longer readily available. Wheatgerm is the nutritious layer between the husk and the grain itself, and is often used in baking to add vitamins and minerals to the diet. Ordinary white flour is made from just the starch and gluten of the grain, with the bran and wheat germ removed. Malted wheat flour has had malted wheat added to it to improve its flavour and texture, and is usually used in bread-making.

Granary flour contains coarsely ground grain. Any type of flour can be ground between stones, in which case it is called stoneground. In early times in Ireland, most grain was ground in water-driven mills, many of which still exist, such as the nineteenth-century example at Annalong in the Mourne mountains, where there were once 20 working mill wheels in the seventeenth and eighteenth centuries. One of the oldest surviving mills is located on the former grain-growing peninsula of Ards, at Ballycopeland in County Down. Built-in the 1780s, it was a working mill until 1915 and has recently been reconstructed. The mill complex includes the miller's house, dust-house and kiln, where the grain is dried before milling. Three sets of mill wheels are still driven on a tributary of the River Clare, near Tuam in County Galway. They were constructed in the seventeenth century and now serve as the focal point of a corn-milling museum.

There were also many windmills built where running water was not available, but few have survived. Blennerville Windmill, near Tralee, was built in around 1800 and remained a working mill until 1880. The five-storey mill has now been renovated to show examples of mill operation from the nineteenth century. This is by no means the tallest existing windmill in Ireland, as the ruins of the mill near Dundalk stand seven storeys high. Tacumshane Windmill was built in 1846, near Wexford, and has also been restored.

There is also an old windmill attached to the Guinness Museum in Dublin, known as St Patrick's Tower. In the home, corn would be ground with a hand-operated millstone known as a quern. Traditionally, breads, muffins, biscuits and cakes, known locally as kets, were cooked on a griddle over the open fire. Breads cooked this way tend to keep longer than those baked in an oven. During the seventeenth century, however, many poorer people substituted potatoes for bread as their staple food, as corn was so expensive. Today's baking delights are more imaginative than those of early times. Herb breads and rolls are lending a flavour of the countryside to the baker's tray. These are made by adding finely chopped fresh herbs and olive oil to the dough. Cheese and onion, and walnut with olive oil breads are also becoming popular in Irish cuisine. Barley, now used in making Irish whiskey, was known to have been cultivated in Ireland as long ago as 3000 BC. The Greek writer Dioscorides wrote that the Irish drank a brew made from malted barley known as curmi, flavoured with herbs. In the Seanchus Mor, a text written in 441 AD, it was recorded that barley was reserved solely for brewing purposes.

The most famous of the Irish beers are, of course, stout, which is given its dark, distinctive colour by adding roasted barley to the brew of sieved, roasted and mashed barley and hops. Oats are one of the earliest of grains to have been cultivated, and closely resemble the original grasses from which they developed. Highly nutritious – containing vitamin B, calcium, iron, protein, fats and carbohydrates – hulled oat grains are ground into fine, medium and coarse oatmeal, which is used extensively in traditional Gaelic cookery and is the basis of porridge. When the grains are passed through heated rollers, rolled oats are produced. Rye is a hardy cereal rarely grown in Ireland and is more common in continental Europe, but it is sometimes used in Irish baking with wholemeal flour to prevent breads becoming stodgy and close-textured.

CLASSIC BOXTY

SERVES 4

Ingredients:

- 225 g/8 oz potatoes, coarsely grated and dried
- 225 g/8 oz potatoes, boiled and mashed
- 2 eggs
- 1 small onion, finely grated
- 2 tablespoons plain (all-purpose) flour
- 3 $1/2$ tablespoons milk
- 1 teaspoon salt
- 1/2 teaspoon freshly ground black pepper
- 50 g/2 oz/$1/4$ cup butter

Directions:

Beat together both types of potato and the eggs, then add all the remaining ingredients except the butter to make a firm mixture. Melt the butter in a large frying pan, then add 2–3 large spoonfuls of the mixture to the pan. Fry the boxties for 3 minutes on each side until golden brown and crisp. Serve immediately with grilled bacon or Apple Sauce.

FARMHOUSE FARLS

'Farl' actually means quarter, so this bread is made in a circle and cut into four.

SERVES 4

Ingredients:

- 450 g/1 lb/4 cups plain (all-purpose) flour
- 3/4 teaspoon bicarbonate of soda (baking soda)
- 1/4 teaspoon salt
- 1/4 teaspoon sugar
- 1 teaspoon corn oil
- 450 ml/3/4 pint/2 cups buttermilk

Directions:

Sift all the ingredients except the oil and buttermilk into a bowl and make a well in the centre. Pour in the oil, then slowly add enough of the buttermilk to mix to a soft dough; you may not need to use it all. Turn out and knead for about 1 minute until smooth, then roll out on a lightly floured board into a thin, flat cake about 23 cm (9 inches) in diameter. Cut a deep cross in the cake, making four farls. Cook the farls for 8 minutes on each side on a moderately hot griddle or in a heavy-based frying pan but be careful not to let them burn. Slit the farls in half and serve with butter or cream and jam.

TRADITIONAL SODA BREAD

Many Irish breads are made with buttermilk, which you can buy in major supermarkets. If you do not have any, simply add a quarter of a teaspoon of lemon juice to ordinary milk.

MAKES one 450 g/1 lb loaf

Ingredients:

- 225 g/8 oz/2 cups wholemeal (whole-wheat) flour
- 300 g/10 oz/2 1/2 cups plain (all-purpose) flour
- 1 teaspoon bicarbonate of soda (baking soda)
- 1 teaspoon salt
- 2 tablespoons unsalted (sweet) butter
- 300 ml/1/2 pint/1 1/4 cups buttermilk

Directions:

Preheat the oven to 200°C/400°F/gas mark 6. Sift the wholemeal flour with 225 g/8 oz/2 cups of plain flour, then stir in the bran remaining in the sieve, the bicarbonate of soda and salt. Rub in the butter, then make a well in the centre. Pour in the buttermilk and stir together to make a crumbly dough. Dust a work surface with the remaining flour, turn out the dough and knead briefly until smooth and elastic. Shape into a roundabout 5 cm (2 inches) thick, dust with flour and cut a 2.5 cm (1 inch) deep cross in the top, almost dividing it into four quarters. Place on a greased baking sheet and bake in the oven for 35 minutes until hollow-sounding when tapped on the base. Cool on a wire rack.

COUNTRY WHITE SODA BREAD

MAKES one 450 g/1 lb loaf

Ingredients:

- 450 g/1 lb/4 cups plain
- (all-purpose) flour
- 2 teaspoons cream of tartar
- 1 teaspoon bicarbonate of soda
- (baking soda)
- 1/4 teaspoon salt
- 2 tablespoons butter, softened
- 1 egg
- 600 ml/1 pint/21/2 cups buttermilk

Directions:

Preheat the oven to 200°C/400°F/gas mark 6. Sift the dry ingredients into a bowl, then rub in the butter. Whisk the egg into the buttermilk, then stir into the dry ingredients and mix to a soft dough. Turn out on to a lightly floured board and knead for 1–2 minutes until smooth. Shape into a circle about 23 cm (9 inches) in diameter, flatten slightly and cut a deep cross in the centre, almost dividing it into four quarters. Place on a greased baking sheet and bake in the oven for 30–40 minutes until hollow-sounding when tapped on the base. Cool on a wire rack.

SWEET IRISH SODA BREAD

MAKES one 450 g/1 lb loaf

Ingredients:

- 450 g/1 lb/4 cups plain
- (all-purpose) flour
- 1 teaspoon salt
- 1/2 teaspoon bicarbonate of soda
- (baking soda)
- 25 g/1 oz/2 tablespoons butter
- 100 g/4 oz/2/3 cup currants
- 1 teaspoon caster (superfine) sugar
- 300 ml/1/2 pint/1 1/4 cups buttermilk

Directions:

Preheat the oven to 180°C/350°F/gas mark 4. Sift the flour, salt and bicarbonate of soda into a bowl, then rub in the butter. Stir in the currants and sugar and make a well in the centre. Pour in the milk and mix to a soft dough. Turn out on a lightly floured board and knead briefly until smooth. Shape into a round, flatten slightly and cut a deep cross in the dough, almost dividing it into four quarters. Place on a greased baking sheet and bake in the oven for about 30 minutes until hollow-sounding when tapped on the base. Cool on a wire rack.

WHOLESOME WHEATEN BANNOCK

MAKES one 450 g/1 lb loaf

Ingredients:

- 450 g/1 lb/4 cups wholemeal (wholewheat) flour
- 4 teaspoons baking powder
- 1 teaspoon bicarbonate of soda (baking soda)
- 1 teaspoon salt
- 75 g/3 oz/1/3 cup butter
- 1 teaspoon finely chopped fresh sage
- 1/2 teaspoon finely chopped fresh thyme
- 300 ml/1/2 pint/1 1/4 cups buttermilk
- 1 egg, beaten
- 1 tablespoon plain (all-purpose) flour

Directions:

Preheat the oven to 180°C/350°F/gas mark 4. Sift the flour, baking powder, bicarbonate of soda and salt into a bowl, then rub in the butter and stir in the herbs. Make a well in the centre, pour in the buttermilk and egg and mix to a soft dough. Turn on to a lightly floured board and knead briefly until smooth. Dust with the plain flour, then turn into a greased 450 g/1 lb loaf tin and bake in the oven for 30 minutes. Reduce the oven temperature to 160°C/325°F/gas mark 3 and bake for a further 15 minutes until hollow-sounding when tapped on the base. Cool on a wire rack.

NOURISHING WHOLEMEAL BREAD

MAKES one 450 g/1 lb loaf

Ingredients:

- 2 teaspoons black treacle (molasses)
- 50 ml/2 fl oz/3½ tablespoons warm water
- 25 g/1 oz/2 tablespoons fresh baker's yeast
- 450 g/1 lb/4 cups wholemeal (wholewheat) flour
- 1 teaspoon salt
- 300 ml/½ pint/1¼ cups warm water

Directions:

Mix together the treacle and warm water, then crumble in the yeast and leave to stand in a warm place for about 10 minutes until frothy. Mix together the flour and salt in a warm bowl and make a well in the centre. Add the yeast mixture and the remaining warm water and mix to a soft, fairly wet dough. Turn out on a lightly floured board and knead briefly until smooth. Turn into a greased 450 g/1 lb loaf tin, cover with a warmed cloth and leave to stand in a warm place for 30 minutes until the dough has doubled in size. Preheat the oven to 190°C/375°/gas mark 5. Remove the cloth and bake the bread in the oven for about 35 minutes until browned on top and hollow-sounding when tapped on the base. Cool on a wire rack.

SIMPLE DROPPED SCONES

MAKES 8–10

Ingredients:

- 225 g/8 oz/2 cups plain (all-purpose) flour
- 1/2 teaspoon bicarbonate of soda (baking soda)
- 1 tablespoon caster (superfine) sugar
- 1 egg, beaten
- 300 ml/1/2 pint/1 1/4 cups buttermilk
- 25 g/1 oz/2 tablespoons butter

Directions:

Mix together the flour, bicarbonate of soda and sugar in a bowl and make a well in the centre. Add the egg and gradually stir in the buttermilk until you have a thick, smooth batter. Heat the butter in a heavy-based frying pan. Drop spoonfuls of the batter on to the hot pan and cook for 2–3 minutes on each side until golden. Remove from the pan and serve warm.

COUNTRY HERB SCONES

MAKES 8–10

Ingredients:

- 225 g/8 oz/2 cups wholemeal (wholewheat) flour
- 2 teaspoons salt
- 1/2 teaspoon bicarbonate of soda (baking soda)
- 50 g/2 oz/1/4 cup butter
- 2 teaspoons dried basil
- 1 teaspoon dried oregano
- 75 g/3 oz/3/4 cup hard Irish cheese, grated
- 1 tablespoon tomato purée (paste) or ketchup
- 1 tablespoon milk
- 150 ml/1/4 pint/2/3 cup buttermilk

Directions:

Preheat the oven to 200°C/400°F/gas mark 6. Sift the flour, salt and bicarbonate of soda into a bowl, then rub in the butter. Stir in the herbs and half the cheese and make a well in the centre. Blend the tomato purée or ketchup into the milk, then add to the flour mixture with the buttermilk and mix to a firm dough. Turn out on a lightly floured board and roll out to 2 cm (1/2 inch) thick. Cut into 8–10 rounds with a pastry cutter, place on a greased baking sheet and sprinkle with the remaining cheese. Bake in the oven for 20 minutes until risen but not hard on top. Serve warm or cool with butter or cream.

BARM BRACK

Barm is the name for the frothy yeast that appears on the top of fermenting malt liquors and ale barm was commonly used as the raising agent for baking in early Irish cookery. This recipe is for a traditional type of cake mix, but often serves as a bread when it is cut into slices and served with butter or cream.

MAKES two 450 g/1 lb loaves

Ingredients:

- 20 g/3⁄4 oz/1 1⁄4 tablespoons fresh yeast
- 150 g/5 oz/2⁄3 cup caster (superfine) sugar
- 300 ml/1⁄2 pint/1 1⁄4 cups warm milk
- 450 g/1 lb/4 cups plain (all-purpose) flour
- 1 tablespoon caraway seeds
- 1 teaspoon allspice
- 1⁄4 teaspoon salt
- 50 g/2 oz/1⁄4 cup butter
- 2 eggs, lightly beaten
- 225 g/8 oz/1 1⁄3 cups sultanas (golden raisins)
- 175 g/6 oz/1 cup currants
- 50 g/2 oz/1⁄3 cup chopped mixed (candied) peel

Directions:

Stir the yeast and 1 teaspoon of the sugar into the warm milk and leave in a warm place for 20 minutes until frothy. Put the flour in a bowl and stir in the caraway seeds, allspice and salt. Rub in the butter and make a well in the centre. Pour in the yeast mixture and the eggs and knead to a soft dough, folding in the fruit. Turn on to a lightly floured board and knead briefly, then place in a greased bowl, cover with a damp cloth and leave in a warm place for 1 hour until it has doubled in size. Preheat the oven to 200°C/400°F/gas mark 6. Divide between two greased loaf tins and bake in the oven for 1 hour. Dissolve the remaining sugar in a little boiling water to make a syrup, then brush this over the warm loaves and return to the oven for 3 minutes to glaze.

Soups and Stews

———

In most peasant societies, the traditional main meal of the day was dispensed from the soup or stew pot which simmered over the stove during the day. There was no real distinction between a soup and a stew, as they were as hearty and robust as the people could afford to make them, adding whatever ingredients were available at the time – hence the expression 'pot luck'.

If a choice of ingredients was available, they would make dishes like the still-famous Dankey stew. 'Dankey' means slightly drunk, so it is not surprising that one of the main ingredients of this stew is a hefty measure of Irish stout. Since this not only adds a rich flavour but also tenderises the meat, it was often added to stews, especially at a time when the water was not always safe to drink and everyone in the family would tend to drink beer of one kind or another. Because most farmers kept cows and made their own butter and cream, these were also common ingredients of soups and stews.

During the Great Famine, soup kitchens proliferated throughout Ireland and many people relied entirely on their daily quota of this free soup for survival when their potato crops were hit by the blight. It was Alexis Soyer, the chef at London's Reform Club in Pall Mall, London, who wrote the official recipe for the universally dispensed soup. During 1848 alone, a total of 8,750 men, women and children were sustained daily on Soyer's soup.

TRADITIONAL POTATO SOUP

SERVES 4

Ingredients:

- 50 g/2 oz/1⁄4 cup butter
- 2 onions, sliced
- 900 g/2 lb potatoes, sliced
- 1 carrot, sliced
- 1.2 litres/2 pints/5 cups stock
- 600 ml/1 pint/2 1⁄2 cups milk
- 1 bay leaf
- 1 teaspoon chopped fresh parsley
- 1⁄2 teaspoon chopped fresh thyme
- salt and freshly ground black pepper
- 2 tablespoons single (light) cream
- 1 tablespoon finely chopped chives

Directions:

Melt the butter in a large saucepan and gently fry the onions until translucent. Add the potatoes and carrot, then stir in the stock and milk. Add the bay leaf, parsley and thyme, and season with salt and pepper. Bring to a simmer, then simmer gently for about 1 hour. Discard the bay leaf and liquidize the soup, then return it to the pan and reheat. Serve with a swirl of cream and garnish with the chives.

LEEK AND OATMEAL BROTH

SERVES 4

Ingredients:

- 600 ml/1 pint/2 1/2 cups milk
- 25 g/1 oz/2 tablespoons butter
- 2 tablespoons oatmeal
- 3 large leeks, cut into chunks
- 1/2 teaspoon salt
- 1/4 teaspoon white pepper
- 1/2 tablespoon chopped fresh parsley

Directions:

Place the milk and butter in a large saucepan and heat until the butter has melted. Stir in the oatmeal and simmer for 1 minute, stirring continuously, then add the leeks, salt and pepper. Cover and simmer over a low heat for about 40 minutes. Add the parsley and simmer for a further 3 minutes before serving.

BLUE CHEESE SOUP

SERVES 4

Ingredients:

- 2 teaspoons vegetable oil
- 6 streaky bacon rashers (slices), rinded and chopped
- 3 shallots, chopped
- 1 large courgette (zucchini), sliced
- 3 potatoes, diced
- 1.2 litres/2 pints/5 cups stock
- 75 g/3 oz/3⁄4 cup blue Irish cheese, crumbled
- 150 ml/1⁄4 pint/2⁄3 cup single (light) cream
- 1⁄4 teaspoon freshly ground black pepper
- 2 tablespoons finely chopped fresh parsley

Directions:

Heat the oil in a large saucepan and gently sauté the bacon for 1 minute. Add the shallots, courgette and potatoes, cover the pan and cook gently for about 15 minutes until the vegetables are soft. Stir in the stock, bring to the boil, then simmer for 10 minutes. Remove from the heat and leave to cool slightly. Liquidize the soup, then return it to the saucepan. Stir in the cheese and cream and heat through gently. Sprinkle with pepper and serve garnished with the parsley.

IRISH NETTLE SOUP

SERVES 4

Ingredients:

- 25 g/1 oz/2 tablespoons butter
- 1 onion, finely chopped
- 2 potatoes, finely chopped
- 450 g/1 lb nettle tips, well washed
- 375 ml/13 fl oz/1 1/2 cups vegetable stock
- 250 ml/8 fl oz/1 cup milk
- 1 teaspoon salt
- 1/2 teaspoon freshly ground black pepper
- 6 tablespoons single (light) cream

Directions:

Melt the butter in a large saucepan and cook the onion and potatoes for about 5 minutes until soft, stirring occasionally. Add the washed nettles and cook for 3 minutes until the leaves wilt, stirring the ingredients together. Stir in the stock, milk, salt and pepper. Bring to the boil, cover and simmer for 15 minutes until the potatoes are tender. Liquidize the soup, then return it to the saucepan and reheat gently. Serve with the cream spooned on top.

POTATO AND CHERVIL SOUP

SERVES 4

Ingredients:

- 75 g/3 oz/1/3 cup butter
- 2 large onions, chopped
- 450 g/1 lb potatoes, diced
- 1.75 ml/3 pints/71/2 cups vegetable stock
- 1 bouquet garni
- 175 g/6 oz fresh chervil
- 1/2 teaspoon salt and white pepper
- 4 tablespoons double (heavy) or whipping cream, whipped

Directions:

Melt the butter in a large saucepan and sauté the onions for about 5 minutes until soft. Add the potatoes, stock and bouquet garni and bring to the boil. Chop the stalks from the chervil, add these to the saucepan and simmer for 20 minutes. Remove from the heat, discard the bouquet garni and leave to cool slightly. Liquidize the soup, then return it to the pan. Chop the chervil leaves finely. Reserve a spoonful for garnish, add the rest to the saucepan and season with salt and pepper. Reheat gently and serve with a swirl of cream and a sprinkling of chervil leaves.

CELTIC CARROT SOUP

SERVES 4

Ingredients:

- 50 g/2 oz/1⁄4 cup butter
- 1 large onion, sliced
- 275 g/10 oz carrots, chopped
- 1.2 litres/2 pints/5 cups
- vegetable stock
- 150 ml/1⁄4 pint/2⁄3 cup orange juice
- 1⁄4 teaspoon salt and white pepper
- 1 tablespoon single (light) cream
- 1 teaspoon chopped fresh chives

Directions:

Melt half the butter in a large saucepan and sauté the onion for about 5 minutes until soft. Add the carrots and cook for 2 minutes. Stir in the stock and bring to the boil. Cover and simmer for 30 minutes until the carrots are tender. Leave to cool slightly, then liquidize the soup and return it to the saucepan. Add the orange juice, salt and pepper and bring gently to the boil, stirring in the remaining butter until melted into the soup. Serve garnished with cream and chives.

BRALLION CLAM CHOWDER

SERVES 4

Ingredients:

- 24 Irish Brallion clams, washed
- 4 potatoes, finely diced
- 600 ml/1 pint/2 1/2 cups milk
- 25 g/1 oz/2 tablespoons butter
- 2 tablespoons chopped fresh chives
- 2 tablespoons plain (all-purpose) flour

Directions:

Place the clams in a large saucepan and cover with water. Bring to the boil over a high heat, cover and cook for about 4 minutes just until they open. Discard any that remain closed. Remove the clams with a slotted spoon, remove the shells and dice the meat. Strain the cooking liquor, return it to the pan and add the potatoes, milk and butter. Bring to the boil, then simmer for 30 minutes. Add the chives and simmer for a further 15 minutes. Mix the flour into a paste with a little water, then stir the paste into the soup and stir until thickened. Return the clams to the soup and heat through before serving bubbling hot.

GAELIC SHRIMP CHOWDER

SERVES 4

Ingredients:

- 25 g/1 oz/2 tablespoons butter
- 1 large onion, sliced
- 3 potatoes, sliced
- 150 ml/1/4 pint/2/3 cup boiling water
- 1/4 teaspoon salt
- 1/4 teaspoon freshly ground black pepper
- 600 ml/1 pint/21/2 cups shrimps or prawns, shelled
- 600 ml/1 pint/21/2 cups milk
- 50 g/2 oz/1/2 cup hard Irish cheese, grated
- 1/2 tablespoon finely chopped fresh parsley

Directions:

Melt the butter in a large saucepan and sauté the onion for a few minutes until translucent. Add the potatoes and stir until coated, then add the water, salt and pepper. Bring to the boil, cover and simmer for 15 minutes until the potatoes are tender. Add the shrimps and milk, return to the boil and stir in the cheese and parsley. Simmer gently for 5 minutes, then serve hot.

COCKLER'S SOUP

SERVES 4

Ingredients:

- 48 cockles, scrubbed
- 150 ml/1⁄4 pint/2⁄3 cup stock, wine or water
- 50 g/2 oz/1⁄4 cup butter
- 2 tablespoons plain (all-purpose) flour
- 600 ml/1 pint/21⁄2 cups milk
- 2 celery sticks (stalks), chopped
- 1 tablespoon finely chopped fresh parsley
- juice of 1 lemon
- 1 teaspoon salt
- 1⁄2 teaspoon freshly ground black pepper
- 4 tablespoons double (heavy) cream

Directions:

Place the cockles in a large saucepan with the stock, wine or water, bring to the boil, cover and steam for about 4 minutes, shaking the pan occasionally until the shells have opened. Lift out the cockles with a slotted spoon, remove the meat and discard the shells. Strain and reserve the cooking broth. Melt the butter in the pan, stir in the flour and cook for 1 minute, stirring. Add the strained broth and stir until smooth. Add the milk, celery, parsley, lemon juice, salt and pepper. Bring to the boil and cook over a low heat for 8 minutes, stirring occasionally. Add the cockles and cook for 3 minutes. Serve with a dash of cream on top.

EIRAAN LAMB AND CHEESE SOUP

SERVES 4

Ingredients:

- 900 g/2 lb lamb chops on the bone
- 1 large onion, finely chopped
- 3 garlic cloves, finely chopped
- 2 bay leaves
- 1.2 litres/2 pints/5 cups water
- 25 g/1 oz/2 tablespoons butter
- 25 g/1 oz/1⁄4 cup plain (all-purpose) flour
- 1.2 litres/2 pints/5 cups milk
- 100 g/4 oz/1 cup Irish Farmhouse cheese, grated
- 4 carrots, diced
- 2 leeks, finely chopped
- 3 potatoes, diced
- 1⁄2 teaspoon salt
- 1⁄2 teaspoon freshly ground black pepper
- 1⁄2 tablespoon chopped fresh chives

Directions:

Put the chops, onion, garlic, bay leaves and water in a large saucepan, bring to the boil, then cover and simmer for 1 hour. Remove the chops from the pan, discard the bones and cut the meat into small pieces. Strain and reserve the stock, discarding the vegetables. Melt the butter in a clean saucepan, stir in the flour and cook for 1 minute, stirring continuously. Stir in the milk, bring to the boil, then simmer for 2 minutes, stirring. Add the reserved lamb and stock, the cheese and vegetables, return to the boil, then simmer for 30 minutes, stirring occasionally. Season with salt and pepper and serve sprinkled with chives.

CROFTER'S HAM, BACON AND BEAN SOUP

SERVES 4

Ingredients:

- 225 g/8 oz/1 cup dried haricot (navy) beans, soaked overnight in cold water
- 225 g/8 oz ham hock on the bone
- 1 tablespoon vegetable oil
- 50 g/2 oz streaky bacon, rinded and diced
- 1 large onion, finely chopped
- 3 garlic cloves, chopped
- 2 celery sticks (stalks), chopped
- 2 large carrots, chopped
- 2 bay leaves
- 2 teaspoons ground cumin
- 6 tomatoes, peeled and chopped
- 2 tablespoons balsamic or wine vinegar
- 1.2 litres/2 pints/5 cups water
- 1 teaspoon mustard
- 1 teaspoon black pepper

Directions:

Drain and rinse the beans, then put them in a large saucepan with the ham, cover with cold water, bring to the boil, then cover and simmer for 2 hours. Remove the hock from the saucepan with a slotted spoon. Discard the fat and bones, dice the meat and return it to the saucepan. Heat the oil in a frying pan and sauté the bacon, onion, garlic, celery, carrots, bay leaves and cumin for about 5 minutes until soft. Add to the ham with the tomatoes, vinegar, water, mustard and pepper. Bring to the boil, then cover and simmer for about 1 1/2 hours until all the ingredients are tender.

DANKEY STEW

SERVES 4

Ingredients:

- 3 celery sticks (stalks), chopped
- 2 carrots, sliced
- 2 large scrag end of mutton chops
- 2 onions, quartered
- 1 tablespoon mushroom ketchup
- 600 ml/1 pint/2 1/2 cups Irish stout
- 1/4 teaspoon salt
- 1/4 teaspoon freshly ground black pepper
- 2 potatoes, sliced
- 50 g/2 oz/1/4 cup pearl barley, soaked in a cup of cold water
- 25 g/1 oz/2 tablespoons salted butter

Directions:

Arrange the celery and carrots in the bottom of a large flameproof casserole dish, place the meat on top and finish with the onions. Stir the mushroom ketchup into the stout, then pour it over the ingredients and season with salt and pepper. Cover with layers of potato slices. Bring to the boil, then cover and simmer at the lowest possible heat for about 1 hour, or cook in a preheated oven at 150°C/300°F/gas mark 2 for 1 hour. Add the barley into the stew and cook for a further 1 hour. Stir in the butter and allow it to melt before serving.

RUSTIC LAMB HOT POT WITH PARSLEY DUMPLINGS

SERVES 4

Ingredients:

- 900 g/2 lb shoulder of lamb, trimmed and diced bones from the lamb
- 2 carrots, chopped
- 1 onion, sliced
- 2 small white turnips, chopped
- 4 potatoes, sliced
- 2 celery sticks (stalks), chopped
- 1 leek, thinly sliced
- 1/4 teaspoon salt
- 1/4 teaspoon freshly ground black pepper
- a dash of Worcestershire sauce
- 150 ml/1/4 pint/2/3 cup single (light) cream
- 1/4 white cabbage, finely shredded
- 1 tablespoon finely chopped fresh parsley

For the parsley dumplings

- 100 g/4 oz/1 cup self-raising (self-rising) flour
- 1 tablespoon finely chopped fresh parsley
- 1/4 teaspoon salt
- 1/4 teaspoon freshly ground black pepper
- 50 g/2 oz/1/4 cup shredded suet
- about 3 tablespoons water

DIRECTIONS:

Put the lamb and bones in a large saucepan, cover with cold water and bring to the boil. Skim off the scum that rises to the surface. Add all the vegetables except the cabbage, season with salt and pepper and top up with water. Return to the boil, cover and simmer gently for about 1 hour until the meat is tender. Lift out and discard the bones. Add the Worcestershire sauce. Ladle out 300 ml/1⁄2 pint/1 1⁄4 cups of the liquid and mix it with the cream, then return this to the saucepan and add the cabbage. Simmer for about 10 minutes until the cabbage is heated through.

To make the dumplings, mix the flour with the parsley, salt and pepper, then stir in the suet. Add just enough water to mix to a stiff dough, then shape with floured hands into eight dumplings. Lift the meat and vegetables out of the saucepan with a slotted spoon and keep them warm. Add the dumplings to the liquid, cover and simmer for about 25 minutes until the dumplings are cooked through. Return the meat and vegetables to the saucepan to reheat, then serve in deep plates sprinkled with the parsley.

TRADITIONAL IRISH STEW

SERVES 4

Ingredients:

- 900 g/2 lb scrag end and neck of mutton, chopped into pieces
- 2 tablespoons plain (all-purpose) flour
- 1/2 teaspoon salt
- 1/2 teaspoon freshly ground black pepper
- 3 onions, sliced
- 4 carrots, sliced
- 2 leeks, sliced
- 5 potatoes, thickly sliced
- 1 tablespoon pearl barley
- 1 teaspoon finely chopped fresh thyme leaves
- 1 tablespoon finely chopped fresh parsley
- 900 ml/1 1/2 pints/3 3/4 cups stock
- 1 tablespoon butter, melted

Directions:

Cut the excess fat off the mutton pieces and sauté the fat pieces in a casserole dish until the fat is released. Lift out the remaining fat pieces with a slotted spoon and discard. Season the flour with half the salt and pepper and toss the remaining meat in the seasoned flour. Add them to the dish and fry until browned on all sides. Lift out three-quarters of the meat, leaving a layer of meat at the bottom of the dish. Cover with a quarter of the onion slices, followed by a quarter of the carrots, then a quarter of the leeks. Season with a little of the salt and pepper, then add a quarter of the potatoes. Continue layering and seasoning until all the ingredients have been used, adding the pearl barley and thyme before the final layer of potatoes. Stir the parsley into the stock and pour over the stew, then spoon over the butter. Bring to the boil for 3 minutes and skim off any scum, then reduce the heat, cover and simmer for about 2 hours until all the meat and vegetables are very tender.

SIMPLE IRISH STEW

SERVES 4

Ingredients:

- 1 kg/2 1⁄4 lb middle neck of lamb, cut into chunks
- 2 large onions, thinly sliced
- 1 kg/2 1⁄4 lb potatoes, thinly sliced
- 1 teaspoon finely chopped fresh marjoram
- 1⁄2 teaspoon salt
- 1⁄2 teaspoon freshly ground black pepper
- 1.2 litres/2 pints/5 cups mutton or lamb stock
- 1⁄2 teaspoon finely chopped fresh rosemary
- 1⁄2 teaspoon finely chopped fresh parsley

Directions:

Preheat the oven to 160°C/325°F/gas mark 3. Trim the fat from the lamb pieces. In a large flameproof casserole dish, layer the meat, onions and potatoes alternately, sprinkling each layer with a little marjoram, salt and pepper and finishing with a layer of potatoes. Add enough stock to half-fill the casserole and sprinkle in the rosemary. Bring to the boil, cover and cook in the oven for about 2 hours. Remove the lid, increase the oven temperature to 190°C/375°F/gas mark 5 and return to the oven for 30 minutes to brown the potato topping. Serve sprinkled with parsley.

WHITE IRISH STEW

SERVES 4

Ingredients:

- 1.5 kg/3 lb potatoes, sliced
- 700 g/1 1⁄2 lb mutton chops
- 450 g/1 lb onions, thickly sliced
- 1⁄4 teaspoon salt
- 1⁄4 teaspoon freshly ground black pepper
- 600 ml/1 pint/2 1⁄2 cups lamb stock
- 150 ml/1⁄4 pint/2⁄3 cup milk
- 50 g/2 oz/1⁄4 cup butter, melted

Directions:

Preheat the oven to 150°C/300°F/gas mark 2. Set aside a quarter of the potatoes in salted water. Arrange a layer of potatoes in the base of a greased casserole dish and cover with a layer of meat, then a layer of onion slices. Repeat the layers until all the potatoes, meat and onions are used, seasoning as you go. Pour in the stock and milk, cover and cook in the oven for about 1 3⁄4 hours. Drain the reserved potatoes. Remove the casserole from the oven and cover with a layer of the reserved potatoes. Pour over the melted butter and return to the oven for a further 1 hour until the potatoes are golden.

VEAL CODDLE

SERVES 6

Ingredients:

- 6 veal escalopes
- 25 g/1 oz veal
- 50 g/2 oz cooked ham
- 100 g/4 oz pork sausage meat
- 1 garlic clove, crushed
- 1⁄4 teaspoon salt
- 1⁄4 teaspoon freshly ground black pepper
- 1 egg yolk, beaten
- 11⁄2 tablespoons plain (all-purpose) flour
- 25 g/1 oz/2 tablespoons butter

For the tomato sauce

- 30 g/11⁄2 oz/3 tablespoons butter
- 1 onion, finely chopped
- 400 g/14 oz/1 large can of tomatoes
- 1 garlic clove, crushed
- 1⁄2 teaspoon salt
- 1⁄2 teaspoon freshly ground black pepper

For the cheese sauce

- 50 g/2 oz/1⁄2 cup hard Irish cheese, grated
- 300 ml/1⁄2 pint/11⁄4 cups single (light) cream
- 1 teaspoon arrowroot
- 1⁄2 teaspoon ground turmeric

Directions:

Preheat the oven to 180°C/350°F/gas mark 4. Beat the veal escalopes flat with a rolling pin. Mince together the veal, cooked ham and sausage meat and stir in the garlic, salt and pepper. Shape into six sausages, roll them in the veal slices and tie with cooks' string. Dip in the egg yolk, then in the flour. Heat the butter in a frying pan and sauté for 15 minutes until golden brown. Transfer to an ovenproof dish and cook in the oven for 15 minutes while you prepare the sauces.

DUBLIN CODDLE

SERVES 4

Ingredients:

- 8 thick slices of ham, cut into chunks
- 16 thin pork sausages
- 900 g/2 lb potatoes, sliced
- 4 large onions, chopped
- 4 tablespoons chopped fresh parsley
- 1⁄4 teaspoon salt
- 1⁄4 teaspoon freshly ground black pepper

Directions:

Place the ham and sausages in a large saucepan, cover with water and bring to the boil. Boil for 5 minutes, then strain, reserving the liquid. Return the ham and sausages to the saucepan and cover with layers of potatoes, onions and parsley, seasoning the layers with salt and pepper. Pour over enough of the reserved liquid to cover the ingredients. Bring to the boil, cover and simmer for 45 minutes. Remove the lid and continue to simmer for a further 20 minutes or so until the liquid has reduced by half.

BACON, BEEF AND BEAN CODDLE

SERVES 4

Ingredients:

- 225 g/8 oz/1⅓ cups dried cannellini or other white beans, soaked overnight in cold water
- 1.2 litres/2 pints/5 cups stock
- 1 tablespoon vegetable oil
- 50 g/2 oz streaky bacon, rinded and diced
- 225 g/8 oz shin of beef, diced
- 1 onion, finely chopped
- 3 garlic cloves, chopped
- 3 celery sticks (stalks), chopped
- 2 carrots, chopped
- 2 bay leaves
- 3 teaspoons ground cumin
- 2 field mushrooms, chopped
- 3 tomatoes, peeled and chopped
- 2 tablespoons malt vinegar
- salt and freshly ground black pepper

Directions:

Drain and rinse the beans thoroughly. Place in a pan, cover with the stock, bring to the boil and boil for 10 minutes. Heat the oil in a large saucepan and sauté the bacon, beef, onion, garlic, celery, carrots, bay leaves and cumin for about 5 minutes until soft. Add the beans and stock, the mushrooms, tomatoes, vinegar, and salt and pepper to taste. Bring to the boil, then cover and simmer for 1½ hours until tender. Remove the bay leaves before serving.

BACON AND CABBAGE STEW

SERVES 4

Ingredients:

- 50 g/2 oz/1⁄4 cup butter
- 1 medium-sized cabbage, shredded
- 1.75 litres/3 pints/7 1⁄2 cups stock
- 1 shallot or small onion, finely chopped
- 1 bay leaf
- 1⁄4 teaspoon salt
- 1⁄4 teaspoon freshly ground black pepper
- 4 streaky bacon rashers (slices), rinded and chopped
- 100 g/4 oz pork sausages, sliced into chunks
- 1 eating (dessert) apple, peeled, cored and chopped

Directions:

Melt the butter in a large saucepan, add the cabbage and stir over a low heat for 10 minutes until the cabbage has wilted. Add the stock, shallot or onion, bay leaf, salt and pepper, bring to the boil, then simmer for about 10 minutes until cabbage is tender. Add the bacon and sausages and simmer for a further 10 minutes. Add the apple and continue simmering for 15 minutes. Remove the bay leaf before serving.

SHEBEEN BACON AND POTATO SUPPER

SERVES 4

Ingredients:

- 450 g/1 lb pork sausages
- 8 thick back bacon rashers (slices)
- 1.2 litres/2 pints/5 cups vegetable stock
- 8 potatoes, sliced
- 4 onions, sliced
- 3 tablespoons chopped fresh parsley
- 1/4 teaspoon salt
- 1/4 teaspoon freshly ground black pepper
- 2 teaspoons finely chopped fresh chives

Directions:

Put the sausages, bacon and stock in a flameproof casserole dish, bring to the boil, then simmer for 5 minutes. Add all the remaining ingredients except the chives, and bring back to the boil. Cover and simmer gently for 1 hour, stirring occasionally, until the stew has thickened. Sprinkle the chives over the top and serve immediately.

Seafood

There is evidence from ancient kitchen middens, or large rubbish heaps, around the city of Cork, of a thriving trade in oysters going back to the Stone Age, and the many oyster fairs held throughout the country celebrate a ritual going back to Ireland's earliest settlers. Mussels have similarly been collected for food since ancient times, and the Murphy's International Mussel Fair, held annually in Bantry Bay, celebrates the seafood's long history. Although plentiful in Ireland, mussels are highly regarded in France, especially in the north-west, an area which has long links with Ireland. This is no better demonstrated than at the French Festival, held in July, which celebrates the long cultural links between Dun Laoghaire and Brest in France.

In 1734, a woman known as Molly Malone was buried in St John's Churchyard, south-east of Dublin, at Blackrock. This is said to be the Molly of the famous rhyme, who wheeled her wheelbarrow through Dublin's broad and narrow streets, selling cockles and mussels, 'alive, alive-oh'. At the bottom of Grafton Street in Dublin, there is a statue of the voluptuous Molly, together with her well-stocked barrow. Some of the best mussels in the whole of Ireland are found on the wild coasts of the west of the island, and these are now commercially packaged and exported around the world. The people of County Kildare swear by their local mussels, which come from Bannow Bay, and they buy them by weight in the local markets.

Ireland's coastal waters provide ideal conditions in which clams thrive. To the west of Ireland are the deeps of the Atlantic Ocean, and to the east are the shallower waters of the Irish Sea. Around ten types of native clam are to be found in the seas around Ireland. Most of these are quite small, but the large hardshell clam has been introduced from its native North America into the waters around the south coast of Ireland. In Northern Ireland, the name for the soft-shelled clam – which is the largest of the local species found in Ireland – is Brallion. There are still many cocklers around Ireland's sandy coasts, raking the flats for the sought-after clams and cockles.

The local fishermen around Derrynane harbour in County Kerry have an odd method of ensnaring the delicious razorfish, which bury themselves in the soft sand when the tide goes out. Razorfish have long, thin, sharp shells and usually have to be dug out of the sand with a pronged rake. In Derrynane, the locals sprinkle salt on the sand where small holes reveal the presence of razorfish. The intensity of the salt causes the shellfish to propel themselves out of their lairs, and they are caught as they leap into the air!

Ireland is famous for its oysters, and when Charles Dickens was writing about being 'secret, and self-contained, and solitary as an oyster' in A Christmas Carol, they were the fare of the Victorian poor. Some of Ireland's best and most succulent small oysters come from the areas of Kilcolgan in County Galway, from Galway Bay itself, Kenmare, Clarinbridge off the west coast, and Strangford Lough. A Pacific variety, known as gigas, is also available. Although it is traditional to eat Irish oysters raw with a drop of lemon juice and a thick slice of soda bread, all washed down with a favourite Irish stout, they can be grilled, steamed or sautéed. St Patrick's Day, 17 March, falls conveniently in the middle of the local oyster season. Although a usual serving would be about six to eight oysters per person, Casanova is reputed to have consumed 50 oysters every morning! Whether that confirms their aphrodisiac qualities, you can decide for yourself. Freshly smoked or canned smoked oysters are also on sale in some fishmongers.

Dublin Bay prawns are also known as the Norway lobster. The reddish-orange or pink prawn has a body around 20 cm (8 inches) in length, with long, narrow, striped claws. Dublin Bay prawns do not change colour when cooked, unlike other crustaceans. This marine crustacean, the source of scampi, does not come from Dublin Bay at all, but is found in Atlantic waters. The name comes from the fact that the Dublin fishing fleet sailed into port with a quantity of these prawns mixed in with their catch. The fishermen would then distribute the prawns to itinerant street-vendors as they had no value in the fish markets, so the name came from the bay from where the street-vendors got their wares.

Lobsters are also a delicacy in Irish fish markets and are sold live and fresh, resplendent in their blue-black shells. Lobsters are quite expensive, however, which could be why the famous Irish lobster dish became known as Dublin Lawyer! The shrimp found in the waters around Ireland are brown shrimp and are generally less than half the size of the smallest prawns. However, as with the prawns, shrimp are now highly valued in Ireland. Although strictly speaking it should appear in the vegetables chapter, another Irish delicacy that feels more at home in a chapter about the sea is carragheen, the reddish seaweed which comes in two varieties: stack-house and sloke or slugane (Porphyra umbilicalis). Sloke is known as laver in Wales where they make the jelly-like substance called laverbread. In the National Gallery in Dublin, there is evidence of the reverence that even the Irish aristocracy had for sloke, as one Georgian exhibit isa beautiful silver sloke pot with a long wooden handle.

Another variety of this edible seaweed is called by its Latin name, Porphyra purpurae, which means 'purple giant'. When cooked, this red-tinged seaweed turns a greenish colour. It is often used as a vegetable, or can be added fresh to salads. Sloke is usually sold already boiled for several hours, when it turns out as a dark-green mush. It is then usually cooked again in milk, then pressed to remove as much moisture as possible, making it somewhat like well-cooked spinach. After this, it is finely chopped, mixed or coated with oatmeal, and fried with bacon or in bacon fat until golden brown on both sides. All seaweeds contain gelatinous agar-agar, a thicken-ing agent used as a substitute for gelatine by vegetarians.

Seaweeds will keep for years if dried and bleached, and are said to ease indigestion and aid sleep. Some seaweeds are used in Irish cooking for thickening fish stews and soups. They are usually bought dried, and must be washed and cleaned of grit before cooking. In County Donegal and on the shores of Ulster, another form of edible seaweed is known locally as dulse or dilisk, deriving its Latin name, Palmaria palmata, from its frond-like shape.

MOLLY'S ONION MUSSELS

SERVES 4

I *ngredients:*

- 30 fresh mussels, scrubbed
- 120 ml/4 fl oz/1/2 cup water
- 120 ml/4 fl oz/1/2 cup white wine
- 1 tablespoon butter
- 6 large onions, sliced
- 4 shallots, chopped
- 5 garlic cloves
- 3 potatoes, sliced
- 2 celery sticks (stalks), chopped
- 6 chicory leaves (Belgian endive), chopped
- 1 carrot, chopped
- 1 sprig of thyme
- 1 bay leaf
- 1 sprig of fresh parsley
- 1/4 teaspoon freshly ground black pepper

Directions:

Put the mussels, water and wine in a saucepan over a high heat, cover and cook for about 5 minutes until the mussels open, shaking the pan occasionally. Discard any that remain closed, lift the mussels from the pan with a slotted spoon and strain and reserve the cooking liquor. Melt the butter in a saucepan and sauté the onions for a few minutes until soft. Add the shallots and garlic, then the potatoes, celery, chicory and carrot. Tie the thyme, bay leaf and parsley together with string, then add to the pan with the mussel liquor and season with pepper. Cover and simmer for 1 hour. Remove the lid and return the mussels to the pan to heat through for about 2 minutes before serving.

MACHA'S MUSSELS

SERVES 4

Ingredients:

- 1.5 kg/3 lb fresh mussels, scrubbed
- 3 tablespoons water
- 25 g/1 oz/2 tablespoons butter
- 2 shallots, finely chopped
- 1 bay leaf
- a handful of chopped fresh parsley
- 150 ml/1/4 pint/2/3 cup Irish cider
- 150 ml/1/4 pint/2/3 cup single (light) cream

Directions:

Place the mussels in a wide shallow pan with the water over a high heat, cover and cook for about 4 minutes until the mussels open, shaking the pan occasionally. Discard any that remain closed. Remove the mussels from the pan with a slotted spoon and set aside. Melt the butter in a pan and sauté the shallots, bay leaf and half the parsley for a few minutes until soft. Add the mussels and pour in the cider. Cook over a high heat for 2 minutes, shaking occasionally. Remove from the heat and lift out the mussels with a slotted spoon, reserving the liquor in the pan. Add the cream and simmer gently for a few minutes until reduced and thickened. Arrange the mussels on a serving dish, pour over the sauce and garnish with the remaining parsley.

BUTTERED GIGAS OYSTERS

SERVES 4

Ingredients:

- 24 gigas oysters
- 100 g/4 oz/1/2 cup butter
- 8 slices of hot toast, buttered
- 1 lemon, cut into wedges

Directions:

Open the oysters into a sieve over a bowl to catch the liquor, and pick out any grit or shell from the oysters. Heat half the butter until it is foaming, then toss in the oysters and heat through for about 1 minute. Arrange the buttered toast on a serving plate. Lift the oysters out of the pan and place on the toast. Add the rest of the butter and the reserved liquor to the pan, bring to the boil, then pour over the oysters and serve garnished with the lemon wedges.

DUBLIN BAY PRAWNS IN CARRAGHEEN JELLY

SERVES 4

Ingredients:

- a large handful of carragheen, or Irish seaweed
- 600 ml/1 pint/2 1/2 cups water
- 1 bay leaf
- 2 cloves
- 2 sprigs of fresh parsley
- a pinch of salt
- 6 cooked Dublin Bay prawns (saltwater crayfish)
- 1 teaspoon vinegar
- 2 slices of lemon

Directions:

Soak the carragheen in water for 15 minutes, then drain. Put the carragheen and water in a saucepan with the bay leaf, cloves, 1 parsley sprig and salt. Bring to the boil, then simmer for 1 hour. To prepare the Dublin Bay prawns, twist apart the body and tail, then gently pull the tail meat out of the shell. Remove and discard the intestinal thread from along the back of the meat. Pull open the body and scrape out the yellow meat. Place all the meat in a bowl. Stir the vinegar into the carragheen mixture, then strain it over the prawns. Leave to cool, then chill and set. Turn out on to a serving plate and garnish with the remaining parsley and the lemon slices.

PRAWNS IN COCKTAIL SAUCE

SERVES 4

Ingredients:

- 300 ml/1⁄2 pint/1 1⁄4 cups mayonnaise
- 2 tablespoons double (heavy) cream
- 1 tablespoon tomato ketchup
- 1 teaspoon Worcestershire sauce
- 1 teaspoon lime juice
- 1⁄4 teaspoon Tabasco sauce
- a pinch of salt
- a pinch of freshly ground black pepper
- 450 g/1 lb cooked, peeled prawns (shrimp)
- 1 teaspoon paprika
- 1⁄4 teaspoon cayenne
- 2 limes, quartered

Directions:

Combine the mayonnaise, cream, tomato ketchup, Worcestershire sauce, lime juice, Tabasco sauce, salt and pepper in a bowl and beat until smooth and evenly coloured. Spoon the mixture over the prawns, sprinkle with paprika and cayenne and garnish with the lime quarters.

CLASSIC DUBLIN BAY PRAWN COCKTAIL

SERVES 4

Ingredients:

- 4 tablespoons whipping cream, whipped
- 2 teaspoons malt vinegar
- 2 teaspoons fresh grated horseradish
- 1/2 teaspoon tomato purée (paste)
- 1/4 teaspoon Worcestershire sauce
- 3 drops of Tabasco sauce
- salt and freshly ground black pepper
- 10 cooked Dublin Bay prawn (saltwater crayfish) tails, shelled and chopped
- 8 lettuce leaves
- 8 chicory leaves (Belgian endive)
- 2 sprigs of fresh parsley, chopped
- 1 lemon, sliced

Directions:

Place the cream in a bowl and mix in the vinegar, horseradish, tomato purée, Worcestershire sauce, Tabasco sauce, and salt and pepper to taste to make a sauce. Stir in the prawns. Line four bowls with the lettuce and chicory leaves, then spoon in the prawn mixture and garnish with the parsley and lemon slices.

DUBLIN LAWYER

SERVES 4

Ingredients:

- 1 fresh lobster, about 1.25 kg/2 1⁄2 lb in weight
- 75 g/3 oz/1⁄3 cup butter
- 4 tablespoons Irish whiskey
- 250 ml/8 fl oz/1 cup single (light) cream
- 1⁄4 teaspoon salt
- 1⁄4 teaspoon freshly ground black pepper

Directions:

If you buy a live lobster, cover the tail with a cloth and hold it firmly on a board. Insert a sharp knife into the cross at the centre of the head and press through to the board. The lobster will be killed instantly. Cook the lobster in boiling water until it turns pink. Once cooled, place back-upwards on a board and cut lengthways through both body and head. Twist off the legs and claws. Remove and discard the head sac and the dark thread from the body and tail. Remove the meat from the body as well as the green liver and the red coral roe in the female. Reserve and clean the half shells. Crack the claws with a hammer and remove the meat using a skewer. Cut all the meat into chunks.

Heat the butter until foaming in a heavy-based pan. Add the lobster meat to the pan and cook lightly for about 4 minutes. Warm the whiskey, pour over the pan and ignite, then leave until the flames die down. Pour in the cream and heat through gently for a few minutes, without allowing the sauce to boil. Spoon the meat into the half shells and pour over the sauce. Season with salt and pepper and serve hot.

POTTED IRISH CRAB

SERVES 4

Ingredeints:

- 900 g/2 lb cooked crab
- 1 teaspoon lemon juice
- 1/4 teaspoon allspice
- 1/4 teaspoon cayenne
- 1/4 teaspoon salt
- 1/4 teaspoon freshly ground black pepper
- 225 g/8 oz/1 cup unsalted (sweet) butter
- 2 tablespoons clarified butter

Directions:

Lay the crab on its back on a board and twist off the claws and legs. Putting the pressure of two thumbs behind and under the body of the crab between its top shell and hard tail parts, lever the body from the shell. Discard the 'dead men's fingers' from the side of the body, the stomach sac in the top of the shell, and any green or spongy substance left in the shell. Scoop out the meat remaining in the shell, keeping the white and brown-coloured meat separate, then cut the body in two and extract any remaining meat with a skewer. Press on the small mouth-part of the crab's body and this should snap away. Crack the claws and legs and scoop out the meat from the sides of the shell.

Preheat the oven to 180°C/350°F/gas mark 4. Season both types of meat with the lemon juice, allspice, cayenne, salt and pepper. Spoon the meat in alternate layers into ramekin dishes. Melt the butter, then pour it gently over the meat in the ramekins, letting it soak into the meat. Stand the ramekin dishes in a roasting tin and fill with boiling water to come half way up the sides of the dishes. Bake in the oven for 25 minutes, then remove from the bain-marie and leave to cool. Pour over the clarified butter to seal the top. Serve with brown bread and butter.

Fish

Although the Emerald Isle is surrounded by seas teeming with fish and other edible seafood, fish recipes are few and far between; until recently, the Irish have generally preferred meat and vegetable dishes to fish meals, even during the Great Potato Famine in the mid-nineteenth century. However, Ireland does have a long tradition of fishing, and today there are a number of significant fishing ports, including Ardglass, Kilkeel and Portavogie.

The traditional fishing vessel unique to the west coast of Ireland is the currach, which dates back thousands of years. These high-prowed boats are shaped like a large canoe and are made from a wooden frame covered with tarred cloth. They are still made to the traditional design in the sleepy little fishing village of Ballydavid in County Kerry. In some places, the rounded coracle – constructed in a similar way – is still in use, mainly for fishing on rivers or lakes.

You will find fish served as you travel around the island, however, and they will often be called by their Gaelic names. It is always nice to know a few local words when travelling in a foreign country and it is especially useful to have some of these names to hand when eating fish in the more remote parts of Ireland – although you may still find the pronunciation difficult. In Irish, the common cod is known as trosc, and codling, or small cod, are often used as they are common in Irish waters. Because they are so versatile, you can find them cooked in all sorts of ways – baked, fried, grilled, poached or steamed – and they are at their best from May until October.

Flounder, the tasty flat fish, is known as fluke in Ireland and is commonly caught in the shallows and rock pools of the west. Plaice are known as leathog, and the brill is broit. Crudan is gunard, while wrasse are known as ballach, both conger eel and the common eel are called eascu, and ling goes by the name of longa. In Gaelic, the whiting is faoitin, and in Northern Ireland, the scad is known as crake herring. The oily mackerel, or ronnach, is at its best between October and March and can often be found on Irish menus either grilled, fried, baked or steamed.

Haddock are locally known as cadog, and at one time, the haddock caught in Dublin Bay were as famous and sought after as its prawns. Salting tends to ruin the delicate flavour of the haddock, so the Irish preserved them by drying and smoking. In some places, haddock was traditionally sun-dried. An old Irish remedy for toothache goes back to the loaves and fishes of Biblical times. It is said that to carry two haddock jawbones in your pocket is a potent preventative against toothache; the older the bones, the more powerful the magic. From the Middle Ages until the late 1700s, Ireland exported vast quantities of salted fish to the Continent.

These were mainly herrings, cadan, cod from Munster and Connaught, and salmon, bradan, salted and exported from a large fishery in Galway. The fish were gutted, then packed in barrels according to their size and quality. Salmon trout, sea trout and brown trout are commonly called breac geal, and a variety of traditional salmon and trout dishes can be tasted at the Limerick Food Festival in June, the Kinsale International Gourmet Festival in October, or the Ballina Salmon Festival. Salmon has always been highly regarded in Irish cuisine and smoked salmon is a particular specialty. There are more than 20 major producers of smoked wild and farmed salmon and trout in Ireland, and most use the traditional peat or oak smoking methods. Some, such as Arran Salmon, offer such delicacies as salmon smoked with truffles or wild garlic.

IRISH TROSC BAKE

SERVES 4

I *ngredients:*

- 450 g/1 lb potatoes, thinly sliced
- 450 g/1 lb cod fillet, skinned and cubed
- 1 onion, grated
- 50 g/2 oz mushrooms, sliced
- 1/4 teaspoon salt
- 1/4 teaspoon freshly ground black pepper
- 275 g/10 oz/1 medium can of tomato soup
- 1 tablespoon finely chopped fresh parsley

Directions:

Preheat the oven to 200°C/400°F/gas mark 6. Cook the potatoes in boiling salted water until tender, then drain. Lay the fish in a greased baking dish, top with onion, mushrooms and a layer of potato slices. Season with salt and pepper. Pour the soup over the potatoes. Bake in the oven for about 25 minutes until cooked through and bubbling hot. Serve sprinkled with the parsley.

COCKLED CODLING

SERVES 4

Ingredeints:

- 3 small onions, sliced
- 6 potatoes
- 700 g/ 1 1⁄2 lb codling fillets
- 1 tablespoon finely chopped fennel
- 1⁄2 teaspoon finely chopped fresh thyme
- a pinch of salt
- a pinch of freshly ground black pepper
- 24 cockles, cleaned
- 25 g/ 1 oz/2 tablespoons butter, melted
- 1 tablespoon finely chopped fresh parsley
- 1⁄2 lemon, sliced

Directions:

Preheat the oven to 200°C/400°F/gas mark 6. Place the onion slices in a saucepan, cover with water and bring to the boil. Simmer for about 3 minutes until softened, then drain. Cook the potatoes in boiling water until tender, then drain and halve. Arrange the fish in a baking dish and sprinkle with the fennel, thyme, salt and pepper. Place the cockles in a large saucepan, cover with water and bring to the boil. Boil until the shells open, discarding any that remain closed. Lift the cockles from the liquid, remove them from their shells and add them to the fish. Strain the juice from the cockle pan over the fish. Arrange the onions and potatoes around the fish, then spoon over the melted butter. Bake in the oven for 15 minutes, basting occasionally, until cooked through and bubbling hot. Serve sprinkled with parsley and garnish with lemon slices.

HADDOCK IN CIDER

SERVES 4

Ingredeints:

- 6 haddock fillets, skinned
- 450 ml/3⁄4 pint/2 cups dry cider
- 1⁄4 teaspoon salt
- 1⁄4 teaspoon freshly ground black pepper
- 50 g/2 oz/1⁄4 cup butter
- 100 g/4 oz mushrooms, sliced
- 1⁄2 tablespoon plain (all-purpose) flour
- 1 tablespoon milk
- 2 teaspoons chopped fresh dill (dillweed)

Directions:

Lay the fillets in a flameproof baking dish, pour over the cider and season with salt and pepper. Bring to a simmer, then cover and poach gently for about 10 minutes until the fish is cooked. Melt half the butter in a separate pan and sauté the mushrooms until soft, then remove the mushrooms from the pan and keep them warm. Add the rest of butter to the pan, then stir in the flour and milk to make a paste. Remove the fish from the heat and strain off the cooking liquor into the second pan. Whisk together to make a sauce, mix in the dill and cook for 2 minutes, stirring. Arrange the mushrooms over the fish, then pour on the sauce. Brown under a hot grill until golden and bubbling.

CODDLED MONKFISH

SERVES 4

Ingredients:

- 2 x 175 g/6 oz monkfish fillets
- 250 ml/8 fl oz/1 cup milk
- 1 onion, sliced
- 1 tablespoon butter
- 1 egg, separated
- 450 g/1 lb mashed potatoes
- 4 sprigs of fresh parsley
- 2 lemons, cut into wedges

For the sauce

- 3 tablespoons brown breadcrumbs
- 25 g/1 oz/2 tablespoons butter, melted
- 2 teaspoons lemon juice
- 1 tablespoon finely chopped fresh parsley
- 1/2 teaspoon dried tarragon
- 1/2 teaspoon dried dill (dillweed)
- salt and freshly ground black pepper

Directions:

Preheat the oven to 180°C/350°F/gas mark 4. Combine the sauce ingredients into a paste. Place one fillet in the bottom of a greased baking dish. Smear the paste over the fillet and place the other fillet on top. Pour the milk around the fish and arrange onion slices on top. Cover with baking foil and bake in the oven for 30 minutes. Meanwhile, mix the butter and egg yolk into the mashed potatoes, then beat the egg white until stiff and fold it into the potatoes. Remove the fish from the oven and cover with potato mix. Bake for a further 15 minutes until the top is lightly browned. Serve garnished with the parsley and lemon wedges.

TARRAGON FLUKE

SERVES 4

Ingredeints:

- 4 flounder fillets
- 2 tablespoons finely chopped tarragon leaves
- 2 tablespoons lemon juice
- 1 garlic clove, crushed
- 75 g/3 oz/1⁄3 cup butter
- 1 tablespoon plain (all-purpose) flour
- 1⁄4 teaspoon salt
- 1⁄4 teaspoon freshly ground black pepper
- 1 teaspoon vegetable oil

Directions:

Place the fish in a glass or ceramic bowl. Mix half the tarragon with the lemon juice and garlic, sprinkle over the fish and leave to marinate for 30 minutes. Heat half the butter in a frying pan until the foam subsides. Season the flour with salt and pepper. Lift the fish from the marinade and coat in the seasoned flour. Turn the fish in the hot butter until coated, then cook for about 5 minutes until cooked through. Mix the remaining tarragon leaves with the remaining butter and the oil and shape into two butter pats. Place the cooked fish on a serving plate and top with the tarragon butter.

CADOG COBBLER

SERVES 4

Ingredients:

- 700 g/1 1/2 lb haddock fillets, skinned and cut into chunks
- 225 g/8 oz/2 cups plain (all-purpose) flour
- 1 teaspoon baking powder
- a pinch of salt
- 50 g/2 oz/1/4 cup butter
- 75 g/3 oz/3/4 cup medium Irish cheese, grated
- 1 egg yolk
- 3 tablespoons milk

For the sauce

- 600 ml/1 pint/2 1/2 cups Béchamel Sauce
- 1/2 teaspoon mustard powder
- 2 teaspoons milk
- 175 g/6 oz/1 1/2 cups hard Irish cheese, finely grated

Directions:

Preheat the oven to 200°C/400°F/gas mark 6. To make the sauce, heat the béchamel sauce to below boiling. Mix the mustard to a paste with the milk, then stir it into the sauce with the cheese and heat very gently until blended. Set aside. Arrange the fish in a greased baking dish and pour the cheese sauce over the fish. Mix together the flour, baking powder and salt, then rub in the butter and stir in half the cheese. Mix to a dough with the egg yolk and milk. Roll out on a lightly floured board and cut into 5 cm (2 inch) rounds with a pastry cutter. Arrange the scones over the fish and brush the tops with milk. Sprinkle the rest of the cheese over the top. Bake in the oven for about 30 minutes until the fish is cooked through and the scone topping is golden brown.

STUFFED LEATHOG

SERVES 4

Ingredients:

- 2 x 350 g/12 oz plaice fillets
- 1 onion, sliced
- 250 ml/8 fl oz/1 cup milk
- 1 tablespoon butter
- 1 egg, separated
- 6 potatoes, boiled and mashed
- 1 tablespoon chopped fresh parsley
- 300 ml/1⁄2 pint/1 1⁄4 cups Parsley Sauce

For the stuffing

- 3 tablespoons fresh breadcrumbs
- 25 g/1 oz/2 tablespoons butter
- 1⁄2 teaspoon dried mixed herbs
- 1⁄4 teaspoon freshly ground black pepper

Directions:

Preheat the oven to 200°C/400°F/gas mark 6. Place one fish fillet skin-side down in a greased baking dish. Mix together the stuffing ingredients and spread over the fillet. Lay the second fillet skin-side up on the top. Spread the onion slices over the top, then pour in the milk. Cover with greaseproof paper and cook in the oven for 30 minutes. Mash the butter and egg yolk into the potatoes. Fold in the egg white, and spread the mixture over the fish. Return to the oven for about 15 minutes until golden brown. Garnish with parsley and serve with parsley sauce.

TIPSY CADAN

SERVES 4

Ingredients:

- 2 carrots, sliced
- 2 onions, chopped
- 1 garlic clove, finely chopped
- 2 teaspoons finely chopped fresh parsley
- 1/4 teaspoon dried thyme
- 1 bay leaf
- 4 peppercorns
- 3 cloves
- 600 ml/1 pint/2 1/2 cups Irish stout
- 10 small herrings
- 1 onion, sliced into rings
- 300 ml/1/2 pint/1 1/4 cups light ale
- 1 tablespoon vinegar
- salt and freshly ground black pepper

Directions:

Preheat the oven to 190°C/375°F/gas mark 5. Mix the carrots, chopped onions, garlic, herbs and spices in a saucepan. Pour in the stout and bring to the boil, then simmer for about 10 minutes until the vegetables are cooked. Turn out into a large baking dish, arrange the herrings on top and cover with onion rings. Pour in the light ale and vinegar and season with salt and pepper. Bake in the oven for 20 minutes until the fish is cooked through. Leave to cool, then serve with Irish soda bread.

RONNACH IN GOOSEBERRY SAUCE

SERVES 4

Ingredients:

- 50 g/2 oz/1⁄4 cup butter, melted
- 1 large onion, finely chopped
- 450 g/1 lb gooseberries, halved
- salt and freshly ground black pepper
- 2 tablespoons fresh breadcrumbs
- 4 x 450 g/1 lb mackerel fillets
- 1⁄2 teaspoon finely chopped fresh fennel fronds
- 2 tablespoons caster (superfine) sugar
- 2 tablespoons water
- 1⁄2 teaspoon grated lemon rind

Directions:

Preheat the oven to 200°C/400°F/gas mark 6. Melt the butter in a small saucepan and sauté the onion for about 5 minutes until soft. Add half the gooseberries, season with salt and pepper, and cook for 5 minutes. Remove from the heat and stir in the breadcrumbs. Spread the paste on the flat mackerel fillets, sprinkle with fennel, then roll them up. Place them on a greased baking dish and bake in the oven for 20 minutes. Place the remaining gooseberries in a saucepan with the sugar, water and lemon rind, bring to the boil, then simmer for about 10 minutes until soft. Purée in a blender. Serve the rolled fillets with the sauce poured over.

VIKING SALMON

SERVES 4

Ingredients:

- 1.5 kg/3 lb salmon
- 3 tablespoons chopped fresh dill (dillweed)
- 1 1/2 tablespoons caster (superfine) sugar
- 4 tablespoons salt
- 2 tablespoons white peppercorns, crushed

Directions:

Clean the salmon, slice in half lengthways and de-bone. Place one salmon piece skin-side down in a casserole dish and sprinkle with the dill. Mix together the sugar, salt, and peppercorns and sprinkle over the dill. Place the second salmon piece skin-side up on top. Place a large plate on the top of the salmon and place some heavy weights on the plate to weigh the salmon down. Put the dish in a refrigerator for 12 hours. Remove from the refrigerator, turn the salmon over, and replace the plate and weights. Replace in the refrigerator for a further 12 hours. Repeat this three more times over a three-day period. Once the fish is marinated, scrape off the salt-dill mixture and pat the fish dry on kitchen paper. Slice very thinly and serve with mustard sauce.

FLUTHERED WILD SALMON

SERVES 4

Ingredients:

- 1 x 1.5 kg/3 lb tail of wild salmon
- 5 tablespoons sea salt
- 3 tablespoons Irish whiskey
- 2 tablespoons freshly ground black pepper
- 2 tablespoons soft brown sugar
- 1 tablespoon lemon juice
- 2 tablespoons finely chopped fresh thyme
- 2 teaspoons finely chopped fresh dill (dillweed)

Directions:

Scale, de-fin, and bone the fish, and divide it into two fillets. Mix together the salt, whiskey, pepper, sugar and lemon juice. Sprinkle the thyme and dill in the bottom of a large baking dish, spoon over 3 tablespoons of the whiskey mixture and place one salmon fillet skin-side down on the top. Spoon almost all the rest of the whiskey mixture over the salmon flesh and place the other fillet skin-side up on the top, finishing with the remaining mixture. Cover with baking foil and place a heavy weight on the fish. Leave in a cool place for three days for the marinade to permeate the fish. Remove the fish from the marinade and clean off the marinade. Serve very thinly sliced.

SPINACH-DRESSED SALMON

SERVES 4

Ingredients:

- 4 lettuce leaves, shredded
- 8 slices of smoked salmon

For the dressing

- 50 g/2 oz baby spinach leaves
- 120 ml/4 fl oz/1⁄2 cup vegetable oil
- 1 1⁄2 tablespoons balsamic vinegar
- 1⁄2 teaspoon lemon juice
- salt and freshly ground black pepper

Directions:

Divide the lettuce between four plates and arrange two salmon slices on each one. Purée the spinach, oil, vinegar and lemon juice together, then season with salt and pepper. Pour the dressing over the salmon and lettuce and serve.

COUNTRY HERB TROUT

SERVES 4

Ingredients:

- 1 lemon
- 2 sprigs of fresh tarragon
- 2 sprigs of fresh thyme
- 4 fresh trout
- 50 g/2 oz/1⁄4 cup butter
- 1 tablespoon flaked (slivered) almonds
- 1 small onion, thinly sliced into rings
- 1⁄2 green (bell) pepper, seeded and sliced into thin rings
- 1 tablespoon tarragon wine vinegar
- 3 tablespoons plain yoghurt
- 1 hard-boiled (hard-cooked) egg, finely chopped
- salt and freshly ground black pepper
- 4 sprigs of fresh parsley

Directions:

Squeeze the juice from half the lemon and cut the second piece in half. Place a tarragon sprig, a thyme sprig and a lemon quarter in each trout cavity. Place a piece of greased baking foil on a grill tray and place fish on the foil. Dot with about one-quarter of the butter and cook under a hot grill for 5 minutes. Turn the fish over, dot with one-third of the remaining butter and cook for a further 5 minutes. Toss the almonds in half the remaining butter, then brown them quickly under the grill. Heat the remaining butter in a small pan and sauté the onion and pepper rings for a few minutes until soft. Mix in the vinegar and yoghurt. Stir in the egg, season with salt and pepper and heat through gently. Place the fish on plates and pour over the lemon juice. Spoon the sauce beside each fish and decorate with the sprigs of parsley.

SAUCES FOR FISH

———

Most of the following sauces are traditionally served hot with poached, baked or steamed firm, white fish, although tartare sauce is made a different way and is served cold. Although there are traditional combinations of seafood and sauce, the final choice of which fish or seafood is best served with which sauce is a matter of personal taste.

Many of these sauces are based on the classic béchamel sauce, which was said to have been invented in France in the late seventeenth century, when Louis de Béchamel, Marquis de Nointel and a steward in the household of King Louis XIV, introduced it to the royal table for the first time.

BÉCHAMEL SAUCE

MAKES 600 ml/1 pint/2 1/2 cups

I *ngredients:*

- 1 small onion
- 4 cloves
- 600 ml/1 pint/2 1/2 cups milk
- 6 peppercorns
- 1 bay leaf
- 50 g/2 oz/1/4 cup butter, unsalted
- 50 g/2 oz/1/2 cup plain (all-purpose) flour

Directions:

Stud the onion with the cloves and place in a saucepan with the milk, peppercorns and bay leaf. Bring to the boil, then remove from the heat and leave to stand for 30 minutes. Strain the flavoured milk into a bowl. Melt the butter in a clean saucepan until foaming, then stir in the flour to create a paste and cook for 1 minute, stirring continuously. Remove from the heat and whisk in the milk, then return to the heat and heat gently until the sauce thickens, stirring all the time until the mixture is smooth. Rub through a sieve, if necessary, to eliminate any lumps.

EGG SAUCE

MAKES 600 ml/1 pint/2½ cups

Ingredients:

- 600 ml/1 pint/2½ cups Béchamel Sauce
- 3 hard-boiled (hard-cooked) eggs
- ¼ teaspoon salt
- ¼ teaspoon freshly ground black pepper

Directions:

Remove the yolks from the hard-boiled eggs and use for another recipe. Heat the sauce gently to just below boiling, then remove from the heat. Press the egg whites through a sieve into the sauce, season with salt and pepper, stir well and heat through gently.

PARSLEY SAUCE

MAKES 600 ml/1 pint/2 1/2 cups

Ingredients:

- 2 tablespoons finely chopped fresh parsley
- 600 ml/1 pint/2 1/2 cups Béchamel Sauce

Directions:

Add the parsley to the sauce and heat through gently.

BÉCHAMEL AND MUSTARD SAUCE

MAKES 600 ml/1 pint/2 1/2 cups

Ingredients:

- 1/2 teaspoon mustard powder
- 1 tablespoon malt vinegar
- 600 ml/1 pint/2 1/2 cups Béchamel Sauce
- 1/2 teaspoon lemon juice
- 1 small fresh chilli
- 2 egg yolks
- 175 ml/6 fl oz/3/4 cup double (heavy) cream

Directions:

Mix together the mustard and vinegar to a paste, then mix this into the sauce with the lemon juice and chilli. Bring to the boil, then remove the chilli. Reduce the heat and stir in the egg yolks and cream. Heat the sauce to just below boiling, then serve.

HERRING ROE SAUCE

MAKES 600 ml/1 pint/2 1/2 cups

Ingredients:

- 50 g/2 oz/1/4 cup butter
- 225 g/8 oz soft herring roes
- 600 ml/1 pint/2 1/2 cups Béchamel Sauce
- 1/2 tablespoon mustard
- 1 teaspoon lemon juice

Directions:

Melt half the butter in a small saucepan and cook the roes over a low heat for about 5 minutes until soft. Warm the sauce, then rub the roes through a sieve into the sauce. Stir in the mustard and lemon juice, then add the remaining butter and let it melt into the sauce over a low heat.

TARTARE SAUCE

MAKES 300 ml/1/2 pint/1 1/4 cups

Ingredients:

- 1 egg yolk
- 1 tablespoon wine vinegar
- 300 ml/1/2 pint/1 1/4 cups corn oil
- 2 hard-boiled (hard-cooked) eggs
- 1 teaspoon capers, chopped
- 1 teaspoon finely chopped fresh parsley
- 1 teaspoon chopped fresh chives
- salt and freshly ground black pepper

Directions:

Whisk together the egg yolk and vinegar, then gradually pour on the oil a drop at a time, whisking continuously until the sauce thickens and emulsifies. Remove the yolks from the hard-boiled eggs and rub them through a sieve into the sauce. Rub one egg white through a sieve into the sauce, then stir in the capers, parsley and chives and season with salt and pepper.

Potatoes

Potatoes were first cultivated thousands of miles from Ireland. An indigenous product of South America, they were grown – many thousands of years before the arrival of Europeans – by the ancient Incas, who lived in the high Andes mountains. They used to preserve them in the frosty nights and the hot tropical sun by freeze-drying them into a form called chuno. The cold climate and damp atmosphere of their original home around Lake Titicaca was ideally matched to that of Ireland, which is why potatoes took so well to the Irish conditions. For some reason, the early Spanish naturalists who first came across the potato cross-pollinated its name with that of the Caribbean sweet potato, or batatas, hence the word 'potato'.

Some historians suggest that it was the naval admiral and first slave-trader Sir John Hawkins who first introduced the potato to England in 1563. It was reputedly Sir Walter Raleigh who first brought them to Ireland from his colony in Virginia, USA, in the 1580s. Raleigh was appointed Mayor of Youghal in County Cork until he fell out of favour with Queen Elizabeth I. On her death in 1603, he was imprisoned in the Tower of London by King James I, and beheaded by the axe, which he ruefully called 'a sharp medicine, but an infallible cure!'.

Sir Walter Raleigh met the famous poet Edmund Spenser (1552–99) at Castle Matrix in County Limerick in 1580, and presented him with his New World tubers. Spenser went on to cultivate the first potatoes in Ireland. Raleigh also gave some potatoes to Lord Southwell, who became the first person to devise the open-field method of cultivation in Ireland. The annual Walter Raleigh Potato Festival is still held in Youghal.

In the seventeenth and eighteenth centuries, the potato became the staple diet in Ireland, as under British rule the wealth of Irish dairy produce and cereals were reserved for export to England. Also, potatoes were easy to grow in Ireland's rich soil and therefore soon dominated the local vegetable plots. In the early days, potatoes were cooked in a special, usually three-legged, iron pot over a turf fire, and they were then drained in a wicker basket.

In England, on the other hand, it took the bad northern European grain harvests of the late seventeenth and eighteenth centuries to force people to accept the potato as a regular part of the diet. Even as early as the first famines of the early 1740s, Edmund Burke wrote, 'Whoever travels through this kingdom will see such poverty as few nations in Europe can equal.' By the early nineteenth century, half of Ireland's peasantry had forsaken traditional cultivation.

The forced subdivision of a farmer's smallholding amongst his surviving sons under the conacre system meant that a living had to be eked out from less than an acre of land. As the potato thrived throughout the island, even those areas with poor soil, it was rapidly adopted as the crop of choice. Indeed, many poor people ate nothing else. By 1845, the rapidly growing Irish population numbered eight million people. When a blight struck the potato crops for three years in a row, therefore, the results were disastrous. During the Great Famine of 1845–7, millions of Irish people emigrated to North America to escape starvation, while over 250,000 people died in 1847 alone.

There are several hundred varieties of potatoes grown throughout the world, and the white Irish variety of potatoes known as Solanum tuberosum are said to be among the sweetest and fluffiest anywhere. Arguably the best new potatoes in Ireland are the Comer variety from County Down. The versatility of the potato, whether new or old, gave rise to a wealth of imaginative ways of cooking with potatoes. With protein, vitamins, minerals and fibre, little fat or salt and plenty of easily assimilated starch, they are among the most nutritious of foods.

IRISH CHAMP

SERVES 4

Ingredients:

- 300 ml/1⁄2 pint/1 1⁄4 cups milk
- 100 g/4 oz spring onions (scallions), chopped
- 8 potatoes, boiled and mashed
- 100 g/4 oz/1⁄2 cup butter
- 1⁄4 teaspoon salt
- 1⁄4 teaspoon freshly ground black pepper

Directions:

Bring the milk to the boil with the spring onions, then simmer for about 5 minutes until tender. Mix the milk and spring onions into the mashed potato. Spoon the mixture into eight ramekin dishes. Make an indentation in the centre of each dish of potato. Cut the butter into eight pieces and place one in each of the hollows. Sprinkle a little salt and pepper on each dish and serve.

IRISH POTATO CAKES

SERVES 4

Ingredients:

- 450 g/1 lb potatoes
- 65 g/2½ oz/⅓ cup salted butter
- 1 teaspoon salt
- ½ teaspoon freshly ground black pepper
- 3 tablespoons plain (all-purpose) flour

Directions:

Place the potatoes in a saucepan, cover with water, bring to the boil and simmer for about 15 minutes until tender. Drain, then mash with half the butter, the salt and pepper and mix in the flour. Turn the mixture out on to a floured board and roll out to about 2 cm (¾ inch) thick. Cut into 7.5 cm (3 inch) rounds with a knife or biscuit cutter. Melt the remaining butter in a large frying pan and sauté the potato cakes for about 10 minutes until golden on both sides. Drain and serve hot.

COTTAGE POTATO SCONES

SERVES 4

Ingredients:

- 450 g/1 lb potatoes
- 75 g/3 oz/⅓ cup butter
- 2 teaspoons salt
- 100 g/4 oz/1 cup plain (all-purpose) flour

Directions:

Cook the potatoes in boiling water for about 15 minutes until soft. Drain well, then mash with half the butter and the salt. Work the flour into the potato mash until stiff. Turn out on to a floured board and shape into 12 equal pieces. Roll the pieces into balls and flatten slightly. Heat the remaining butter and sauté the scones for about 5 minutes on each side until browned, then serve hot with butter.

FARMER'S POTATOES

SERVES 4

Ingredients:

- 700 g/1 1/2 lb potatoes, sliced
- 1 tablespoon butter
- 175 g/6 oz streaky bacon, rinded and diced
- 1 small onion, thinly sliced
- 1/2 teaspoon freshly ground black pepper
- 150 ml/1/4 pint/2/3 cup single (light) cream
- 3 tablespoons milk
- 100 g/4 oz/1 cup hard Irish cheese, sliced
- 1 shallot, thinly sliced

Directions:

Preheat the oven to 180°C/350°F/gas mark 4. Cook the potatoes in boiling water for 5–10 minutes until just soft, then drain. Arrange half the potato slices on the bottom of a greased baking dish. Melt the butter and sauté the bacon and onion until soft, then add the pepper. Spoon the bacon and onion mixture over the potatoes. Arrange the rest of the potatoes over the bacon and onion. Mix the cream and milk, then pour this over the top and cover with cheese slices. Dot the shallot slices on top of the cheese. Bake in the oven for about 30 minutes until cooked through and golden on top.

O'BRIEN'S POTATOES

SERVES 4

Ingredients:

- 4 potatoes
- 1 leek, boiled and sliced
- 2 onions, finely chopped
- 2 tablespoons plain (all-purpose) flour
- a pinch of salt
- 6 tablespoons hot milk
- 100 g/4 oz/1 cup mature Irish cheese, grated
- 50 g/2 oz/1 cup dry brown breadcrumbs
- 50 g/2 oz/1/4 cup butter
- a pinch of cayenne

Directions:

Preheat the oven to 180°C/350°F/gas mark 4. Cook the potatoes in boiling water for about 15 minutes, then drain and slice. Mix the potatoes with the leek, onion, flour and salt, then stir in the milk and three-quarters of the cheese. Grease a baking dish and pour in the mixture. Sprinkle the mixture with breadcrumbs, then the remaining cheese. Dot pieces of the butter over the dish and sprinkle with cayenne. Cook in the oven for about 35 minutes until the top browns and bubbles, then serve piping hot.

SAFFRON POTATOES

SERVES 4

Ingredients:

- 900 g/2 lb potatoes
- 1/4 teaspoon salt
- 450 g/1 lb hard Irish cheese, grated
- 1/4 teaspoon freshly ground black pepper
- 3 saffron strands
- 4 tablespoons lamb or chicken stock
- 4 tablespoons single (light) cream
- 40 g/1 1/2 oz/3 tablespoons butter

Directions:

Preheat the oven to 180°C/350°F/gas mark 4. Cook the potatoes in boiling salted water for about 15 minutes until tender, then drain, cool and slice thinly. Arrange a layer of slices in a greased baking dish, cover with a little cheese and a sprinkling of pepper, then repeat until all the potatoes are used, reserving a tablespoon of the cheese. Soak the saffron in a little boiling water, then mix with the stock, cream and remaining cheese. Pour the mixture over the potatoes and dot with the butter. Bake in the oven for 20 minutes until golden brown on top.

APPLE AND POTATO SALAD

SERVES 4

Ingredients:

- 450 g/1 lb new potatoes
- 4 generous sprigs of fresh mint
- 1 green eating (dessert) apple, peeled and cored
- 1 tablespoon lemon juice
- 1 teaspoon mustard
- 1 egg yolk
- 150 ml/1⁄4 pint/2⁄3 cup vegetable oil
- 1 tablespoon dry cider
- 1 tablespoon chopped fresh mint leaves
- 1⁄4 teaspoon salt
- 1⁄4 teaspoon freshly ground black pepper

Directions:

Cook the potatoes in boiling water with 2 sprigs of mint for about 15 minutes until tender. Drain, then quarter. Slice the apple into segments and sprinkle with lemon juice. Make a mayonnaise by beating together the mustard and egg yolk. Gradually whisk in the oil a drop at a time until the mixture emulsifies and thickens. Stir in the cider and chopped mint and season with salt and pepper. Toss the apple and potatoes in the mayonnaise. Chill, then serve garnished with the remaining mint sprigs.

DairyProducts

BUTTER AND CREAM

I reland has always been famous for its rich and creamy butter, as the lush pastures support large herds of productive dairy cattle. The Gaelic word for the greenest grass, watered by a stream, is glasghaibhlinn and this pasture produces the best milk, of which the last and richest part is sniugadh. In the past, farmers used to make their own produce, but now there are numerous large butteries spread across the country, and some are now diversifying into different dairy products, such as butters flavoured with garlic and herbs or other ingredients. Ireland is now the fourteenth largest producer of butter in the world and much of its produce is exported to other countries.

Butter, cream and other dairy products have always been used extensively in Irish cooking. There are two main types of butter. Sweet cream butter is made from fresh cream, while lactic butter is made from ripened cream to which bacterial agents have been added to improve the flavour. This is salted butter. The cream from around ten litres/ 18 pints of milk goes into making just 450 g/1 lb of butter. With a high energy content, butter contains calcium and vitamins A and D. In medieval times, butter was packed into wooden churns and stored in peat bogs. This bog butter, as it was known, has been found in bogs after hundreds of years. It was sadly inedible, but still smelled like and resembled very cold, hard butter.

Buttermilk, locally known as 'bonny clobber', is used extensively in Irish cooking. Although it is now manufactured using a culture, it was traditionally the liquid left over after churning the butter, and it has a distinctive sour flavour. Once quite difficult to buy in the supermarkets, it is again much more readily available, but you can substitute milk mixed with a teaspoon of lemon juice if necessary. The container generally used to carry buttermilk is known in Gaelic as a piggin.

The cream is the part of the milk that contains most of the fat, and the different types of cream have different culinary qualities because of that. Single cream contains 18 per cent butterfat and is used to give a smooth texture and flavour to many dishes, while double cream contains 48 per cent butterfat and is used in richer dishes and for thickening. Another type of cream more usually associated with the West Country of England but also well used in Ireland is clotted cream, and its use probably came over to Ireland from Cornwall. It is made by leaving milk to stand for 12 hours, then heating it gently and skimming off the crusty layer from the top. In Connaught and Ulster, there are still stories of butter fairies who steal the cream from the top of any milk left standing, and leprechauns who turn the milk sour.

IRISH CHEESE

———

Cheese, or cais in Gaelic, is one of our oldest foods and was probably eaten as long as 11,000 years ago. In Ireland, the art of cheese-making dates back at least to the travelling monks of the ninth and tenth centuries, and cheese has been an important ingredient in the Irish diet since early Christian times. Towards the end of the 1600s, however, the art of making cheese went into something of a decline and by the mid-nineteenth century, around the time of the Great Famine, cheese-making in Ireland had almost died out. Over the past few decades, however, the revival in local cheese-making has produced a wonderful selection of cheeses.

Originally a method of preserving milk, cheese is made by curdling milk with rennet, creating a solid, the curds, and a liquid, the whey. The country way of making an Irish cream cheese was by putting thick curds into a cloth and hanging the cloth bag from the roof of the cottage, letting the thin, watery liquid drain out. The remaining cheese was then placed in a hooped, wooden sieve, pressed down and left to mature. Hard cheeses were made by drawing off the curds, which were then pressed, or moulded, salted, drained, dried, cured and aged, then ripened by various methods to produce the different varieties of cheese, all rich in protein, fat, minerals and vitamin A. The flavour of the final product depends both on exactly how the cheese is made and also on the source of the milk – cows, sheep or goats – and on the pasture on which they have grazed.

About 30 farmhouse cheese-makers currently make over 40 different varieties of traditional Irish cheeses but there are around 170 different Irish cheeses altogether, and they vary considerably in texture and strength from the semi-soft derrynaflan cheese to the hard, unpasteurized gigginstown cheese. Dunlop was originally an Irish cheese which was introduced into Scotland by a refugee from religious persecution in the seventeenth century. It is similar to cheddar but with a moist, fine texture. Also similar to cheddar is Ireland's only raw-milk cheese, made by Baylough in Clogheen, Tipperary. Likened to gouda, coolea cheese is a cows' milk cheese with orange rind which is made in County Cork and is ideal for recipes where grated hard Irish cheese is called for.

Another cheese likened to Dutch cheese is ardrahan, also from Cork. The dry and crumbly gabriel cheese is ideal for any recipe that calls for parmesan. Carrigaline Farmhouse produces mild, semi-hard cheeses either natural, or flavoured with garlic and herbs. Friesian cows' milk is used to prepare Riverville Farmhouse cheese in Galway, and three flavours are produced, as well as original: garlic, peppered and spiced.

One of the first Irish blue cheeses to be made in country farmhouses was cashel blue, a cows' milk cheese from Tipperary, which has been compared to gorgonzola. Mileens, a product of West Cork, is a soft, spicy, creamy cheese with the texture of camembert. The rind of this cheese is washed in salt water as it matures. A similar cheese, made in Thurles in County Tipperary, is Cooleeny Farmhouse cheese, with its white mould rind and gooey inside. The cheeses made at the Carrigbyrne Farmhouse are likened to a cross between camembert and brie. One, musky-flavoured Irish cheese is gubbeen, which is made in Skull in County Cork with vegetarian rennet and unpasteurized cows' milk. These ingredients are also used in durrus cheese, a soft variety with a dark pink rind. Produced in Cork, this is a mellow, wholesome cheese. Knockanore Farmhouse also makes a variety of cheeses, including oak-smoked, red, garlic, herb, black pepper and chive-flavoured. These cheeses are hand-turned and individually waxed. Oak smoking is also used by Ardrahan Farmhouse, which also produces a semi-soft, rind-washed traditional cheese. Cahills Farm in

Limerick flavours its cheeses with red wine, porter, whiskey and fine herbs. Carbery, in County Cork, produces a dubliner cheese, and Compsey, of Tipperary, make a cream cheese. Instantly recognized by their surface designs of the shamrock and Celtic motifs, Dunbarr's soft, cows' milk cheese is produced in Dublin.

The many varieties of Irish cheese also include those made with sheep's or goats' milk. One well known goats' milk cheese is inagh, from Shannon, and Corleggy also makes a mature goats' cheese as well as cows' milk cheeses flavoured with garlic, cumin or green peppercorn, or smoked.

TRADITIONAL IRISH RAREBIT

SERVES 4

Ingredients:

- 225 g/8 oz/2 cups hard Irish cheese, grated
- 2 teaspoons cornflour (cornstarch)
- 1 teaspoon mustard powder
- 2 teaspoons white vinegar
- 2 eggs
- 300 ml/1/2 pint/1 1/4 cups milk
- a pinch of salt and freshly ground black pepper
- a dash of Tabasco sauce
- 4 slices of Irish wholemeal (wholewheat) bread
- 1/4 teaspoon paprika

Directions:

Mix together all the ingredients except the bread and paprika in a saucepan. Cook over a low heat, stirring constantly, until the mixture is well blended and hot. Remove from the heat and spread the mixture on the bread slices. Grill under a hot grill for a few minutes until golden brown, then serve sprinkled with a little paprika.

TIPSY DUBLIN RAREBIT

SERVES 4

Ingredients:

- 1 tablespoon butter
- 100 g/4 oz/1 cup hard Irish cheese, finely grated
- 1 teaspoon mustard powder
- 2 tablespoons Irish stout
- 4 thick slices of brown bread
- 1/4 teaspoon cayenne

Directions:

Melt the butter in a saucepan over a low heat, then add the cheese and very gently allow it to melt. Mix the mustard with a little of the stout, then stir it into the remaining stout. Mix this into the cheese and butter. Toast the bread on both sides. Press down on the centre of the toast slices, creating a flat, well shape. Carefully spoon the stout and cheese mixture over the toast and place under a hot grill for a few minutes until browned. Serve sprinkled with the cayenne.

SORREL SOUFFLÉ

SERVES 4

Ingredeints:

- 3 tablespoons milk
- 3 tablespoons white breadcrumbs
- 50 g/2 oz/1⁄4 cup butter
- 450 g/1 lb fresh sorrel, cleaned and chopped
- 2 eggs, separated
- 4 tablespoons grated hard cheese
- salt and white pepper

Directions:

Preheat the oven to 180°C/350°F/gas mark 4. Pour the milk over the breadcrumbs and leave to soak. Melt the butter in a large saucepan, add the sorrel and cook gently for about 3 minutes until the sorrel wilts. Beat the egg yolks, then stir them into the sorrel with the milk and breadcrumbs. Sprinkle the cheese over the base of a greased soufflé dish. Beat the egg whites with a pinch of salt and pepper until stiff, then fold them gently into the sorrel mixture. Pour the mixture into the dish and bake in the oven for about 20 minutes until the top has risen and browned slightly. Serve at once.

CHEESE AND POTATO CAKES

SERVES 4

Ingredients:

- 350 g/12 oz potatoes
- 2 egg yolks, beaten
- 2 tablespoons double (heavy) cream
- 40 g/11⁄2 oz/1⁄2 cup hard Irish cheese, grated
- a pinch of dried basil
- a pinch of cayenne
- 1⁄2 teaspoon salt
- 1⁄2 teaspoon black pepper
- 2 tablespoons plain (all-purpose) flour
- 1 egg, beaten
- 3 tablespoons white breadcrumbs
- 3 tablespoons oil

Directions:

Cook the potatoes in boiling water for about 15 minutes until tender, then drain and rub through a sieve. Beat the egg yolks with the cream, then stir into the hot potatoes. Stir in the cheese, basil and cayenne, and season with salt and pepper. Shape the mixture into small cakes. Coat the cakes with flour, then dip them in the beaten egg and coat with breadcrumbs. Heat the oil in a heavy-based frying pan and fry the cakes for about 10 minutes until golden brown on both sides.

CHEESE AND CHIVE SOUFFLÉ

SERVES 4

Ingredients:

- 4 eggs, separated
- a dash of Tabasco sauce
- 1⁄4 teaspoon salt
- 1⁄4 teaspoon white pepper
- 225 g/8 oz/1 cup cottage cheese
- 2 tablespoons finely chopped fresh chives
- 1 tablespoon finely chopped fresh parsley
- 1 tablespoon butter

Directions:

Preheat the oven to 200°C/400°F/gas mark 6. Beat the egg yolks with the Tabasco, salt and pepper, then beat in the cottage cheese a little at a time. Whisk the egg whites until stiff, then fold gently into the mixture with the chives and parsley. Butter a small flameproof baking dish and heat on the hob until hot. Pour in the mixture and turn the heat down very low. Leave on the heat for about 3 minutes, then transfer to a hot oven for about 10 minutes until the soufflé has risen and browned. Serve immediately.

CHEESE CUSTARD

SERVES 4

Ingredients:

- 250 ml/8 fl oz/1 cup milk
- 100 g/4 oz/1 cup hard Irish cheese, grated
- 2 eggs, beaten
- salt and freshly ground black pepper

Directions:

Preheat the oven to 200°C/400°F/gas mark 6. Heat the milk and cheese in a flameproof, ovenproof pan, stirring until the cheese has dissolved. Stir in the beaten eggs and season with salt and pepper. Transfer to the oven and cook for 15 minutes until set, then serve hot.

FARMHOUSE CHEESE PARCELS

SERVES 4

Ingredients:

- 4 x 15 cm (6 inch) square double sheets of filo pastry
- 4 x 75 g/3 oz slices of hard Irish cheese, cut into rectangles
- 4 x 75 g/3 oz slices of blue Irish cheese
- 4 x 75 g/3 oz slices of soft Irish cheese
- 3 tablespoons butter, melted

For the salad:

- 2 parsnips
- 2 carrots
- 2 courgettes (zucchini)

For the dressing:

- 175 ml/6 fl oz/3⁄4 cup olive oil
- 4 tablespoons red wine vinegar
- 4 teaspoons caster (superfine) sugar
- 4 tablespoons chopped fresh mixed herbs
- 1 egg yolk
- 1⁄2 teaspoon salt
- 1⁄2 teaspoon freshly ground black pepper

Directions:

Preheat the oven to 190°C/375°F/gas mark 5. Place the filo
sheets on the work surface and pile the cheeses on top, one
on top of the other with the blue cheese in the centre.

Moisten the edges of the pastry and seal into small parcels. Brush the parcels with the melted butter. Place seam-side down on a greased baking sheet and bake in the oven for 5–7 minutes until the cheese has melted and the pastry browned. Make a salad by cutting the vegetables into julienne strips and dividing between individual plates. Liquidize all the dressing ingredients, then pour over the vegetable salad. Place a cheese parcel on each plate and serve at once.

BUTTERMILK PUDDING

SERVES 4

Ingredients:

- 1 teaspoon powdered gelatine
- 2 tablespoons water
- 300 ml/1⁄2 pint/1 1⁄4 cups double (heavy) cream
- 150 g/5 oz/2⁄3 cup caster (superfine) sugar
- 1 vanilla pod (bean), halved
- 600 ml/1 pint/2 1⁄2 cups buttermilk

Directions:

Stir the gelatine into the water in a small bowl, then stand the bowl in a pan of hot water until the gelatine is transparent. Place half the cream, the sugar and vanilla pod in a saucepan and heat to just below boiling point. Remove from the heat and stir in the gelatine, blending well. Whisk the buttermilk into the hot cream. Remove the vanilla pod. Whisk the remaining cream until stiff, then fold into the hot mixture. Pour into a bowl, leave to cool, then chill well before serving.

IRISH EGGS BENEDICT

SERVES 4

Ingredients:

- 4 thick slices of cooked ham
- 4 eggs
- 4 thick slices of bread
- 2 teaspoons chopped fresh chives

For the sauce:

- 2 egg yolks
- 2 teaspoons lemon juice
- 150 g/5 oz/2⁄3 cup butter, melted

Directions:

Wrap the ham in baking foil and heat in a low oven. Poach the eggs and keep them warm. Toast the bread and keep it warm. To make the sauce, whisk the egg yolks and lemon juice until creamy, then very carefully and gradually pour in the melted butter, stirring constantly until it thickens. Place a warm ham slice on each of the warm bread slices and place a poached egg on top. Spoon the sauce over the eggs and garnish with the chives.

Vegetables

―――

O ne of the most common ingredients in cookery all over the world is the tomato, which originally comes from the maize fields of the Andes in South America. Originally considered a weed, this herbaceous plant was then grown for its fruit for thousands of years before it was discovered by the conquering Spanish and thence brought to Europe. The tomato (Lycopersicum esculenta) is a member of the Solanaceae family, which includes henbane, nightshade, chillies, peppers, aubergine (eggplant), tobacco and the potato. It grows well in most climates, and adapted itself even to the temperate climate of Ireland. Rich in vitamins A and C, iron and sugar, tomatoes are widely used in Irish sauces, relishes, pickles, chutneys and ketchup.

When it was first brought to Europe in the sixteenth century, the tomato was shunned by many because it was thought to be poisonous and the seeds were believed to cause appendicitis. Not only that, but Cromwell's Parliament believed it to be morally corrupting, and it became known as the pomme d'amour, or love apple. Like the potato and the tomato, maize – or sweetcorn – also arrived in Ireland from the Americas. Before the Great Famine of the nineteenth century, the average household of two adults and four children would eat 11 kg/ 24 lb of potatoes a week and most were almost entirely dependent on potatoes for their food. When the crops failed, the Irish looked to England to provide alternative food for the starving population. All they were offered was a maize meal made from the American corn cob. Many people were saved by making bread with the distinctive yellow flour and it remains a feature of local cooking.

Another native American product that has been introduced into Irish cookery is the sunflower. The oil, which is pressed from the flower's tiny, highly nutritious seeds, is widely used in cookery and sauces, and is light, with a faintly nutty flavour. Hulled sunflower seeds are also eaten raw and are high in protein and carbohydrates.

COLCANNON

SERVES 4

Ingredients:

- 450 g/1 lb potatoes
- 450 g/1 lb curly kale, sliced
- 1 large leek, thinly sliced
- 150 ml/1/4 pt/2/3 cup single (light) cream
- 1/4 teaspoon salt
- 1/4 teaspoon freshly ground black pepper
- 75 g/3 oz/1/3 cup butter, melted

Directions:

Cook the potatoes in boiling water for about 15 minutes until tender, then drain and mash. Cook the kale in a little water for about 10 minutes until soft, then drain and chop finely. Simmer the leek in the cream for about 5 minutes until soft, then stir into the mashed potatoes with the kale and season with salt and pepper. Spoon the warm mixture into a deep dish and make a well in the centre. Pour the melted butter into the centre and serve.

IRISH CAULIFLOWER CHEESE

SERVES 4

Ingredients:

- 1 large cauliflower
- 4 bay leaves
- 50 g/2 oz/1⁄4 cup butter
- 1 large onion, sliced
- 2 tomatoes, peeled and sliced
- 25 g/1 oz/1⁄4 cup plain (all-purpose) flour
- 300 ml/1⁄2 pint/1 1⁄4 cups milk
- 1 teaspoon mustard
- 175 g/6 oz/1 1⁄2 cups hard Irish cheese, grated
- 1⁄4 teaspoon salt
- 1⁄4 teaspoon freshly ground black pepper
- 4 eggs, separated
- 2 tablespoons fresh breadcrumbs
- 2 spring onions (scallions), thinly sliced

Directions:

Break the cauliflower head into florets, cutting out the stem. Steam the cauliflower over boiling water with the bay leaves for about 10 minutes until just tender, then drain and place in a flameproof dish. Melt half the butter and sauté the onion until soft. Add the tomatoes and cook for 3 minutes, then pour over the cauliflower. Melt the remaining butter and stir in the flour. Whisk in the milk, mustard, two-thirds of the cheese, and the salt and pepper. Pour over the cauliflower. Beat the egg whites until stiff, then place four large spoonfuls on top of the sauce. Make an indentation in each mound of egg white and fill them with the egg yolks. Scatter the breadcrumbs over the dish, then the rest of the cheese and the spring onions. Place under a hot grill for a few minutes until golden brown.

POTATO AND PARSNIP BAKE

SERVES 4

Ingredients:

- 450 g/1 lb potatoes, sliced
- 1 large onion, sliced
- 225 g/8 oz parsnips, sliced
- 50 g/2 oz/1⁄4 cup butter
- 1⁄2 teaspoon salt
- 1⁄2 teaspoon freshly ground black pepper
- 300 ml/1⁄2 pint/11⁄4 cups milk or buttermilk

Directions:

Preheat the oven to 180°C/350°F/gas mark 4. Arrange the vegetables in layers in a greased baking dish, dotting each layer with a little butter and seasoning with salt and pepper. Finish with a layer of potatoes. Pour over the milk or buttermilk, cover and bake in the oven for 11⁄2 hours. Remove the cover and bake for a further 30 minutes to brown the potatoes.

LEEK AND POTATO CASSEROLE

SERVES 4

Ingredients:

- 450 g/1 lb potatoes, thinly sliced
- 450 g/1 lb leeks, cut into
- 4 cm (1 1/2 inch) slices
- 40 g/1 1/2 oz/3 tablespoons butter
- 25 g/1 oz/1/4 cup wholemeal (wholewheat) flour
- 300 ml/1/2 pint/1 1/4 cups milk
- 1/2 teaspoon mustard powder
- 1/4 teaspoon freshly ground black pepper
- 50 g/2 oz/1/2 cup hard Irish cheese, grated

Directions:

Preheat the oven to 200°C/400°F/gas mark 6. Cook the potatoes in boiling water for about 5 minutes until tender, then drain. Steam the leeks for about 10 minutes until just tender. Arrange the potatoes and leeks in a greased casserole dish. Melt the butter in a saucepan, stir in the flour and cook for 2 minutes, stirring, then whisk in the milk, mustard and pepper and cook over a low heat until thickened. Pour the sauce over the casserole and sprinkle with cheese. Bake in the oven for about 20 minutes until golden brown.

PARSNIP, CELERIAC AND POTATO MASH

SERVES 4

Ingredients:

- 350 g/12 oz potatoes, roughly chopped
- 225 g/8 oz celeriac, roughly chopped
- 225 g/ 8 oz parsnips, roughly chopped
- 175 ml/6 fl oz/3⁄4 cup milk
- 1⁄2 teaspoon mustard
- salt and freshly ground black pepper
- 75 g/3 oz/1⁄3 cup butter

Directions:

Place the vegetables in a saucepan and cover with cold water. Bring to the boil, then simmer for about 10 minutes until the potatoes are cooked. Drain well, then return them to the saucepan, add the milk, mustard and salt and pepper and mash together until smooth. Place over a low heat, add the butter and stir until it has melted into the vegetables.

CIDER ONION BAKE

SERVES 4

Ingredients:

- 50 g/2 oz/1/4 cup butter
- 4 onions, halved crossways
- 1 teaspoon dried thyme
- 1/2 teaspoon dried sage
- 1/2 teaspoon dried marjoram
- 1/4 teaspoon salt
- 1/4 teaspoon freshly ground black pepper
- 4 tablespoons cider
- 1 teaspoon finely chopped fresh sage

Directions:

Preheat the oven to 180°C/350°F/gas mark 4. Melt the butter in a flameproof, shallow casserole dish and sauté the onions flat-side down until browned. Remove from the heat, turn the onions flat-side up and sprinkle with thyme, sage, marjoram, salt and pepper. Pour the cider into the dish, cover and bake in the oven for 1 hour until tender, spooning the cooking liquid over the onions from time to time. Serve sprinkled with fresh sage.

PARSNIP BAKE

SERVES 4

Ingredients:

- 450 g/1 lb parsnips, quartered
- 250 ml/8 fl oz/1 cup lamb or chicken stock
- a pinch of nutmeg
- salt and freshly ground black pepper
- 25 g/1 oz/2 tablespoons butter

Directions:

Preheat the oven to 180°C/350°F/gas mark 4. Cook the parsnips in boiling water for about 15 minutes until half-cooked, then drain and place in an ovenproof dish. Add the stock and nutmeg and season with salt and pepper. Dot with the butter, then bake in the oven for 30 minutes until tender and golden brown.

BRAISED IRISH CELERY

SERVES 4

Ingredients:

- 100 g/4 oz streaky bacon, rinded
- 1 onion, sliced
- 1 carrot, sliced
- 10 celery sticks (stalks), without the leaves, cut into large chunks
- 300 ml/1⁄2 pint/1 1⁄4 cups chicken stock
- 1 bouquet garni
- 1⁄4 teaspoon salt
- 1⁄4 teaspoon freshly ground black pepper

Directions:

Arrange the bacon in the bottom of a flameproof casserole dish and add the onion, carrot and celery. Pour in the stock, then add the bouquet garni, salt and pepper. Bring to the boil, cover and simmer gently for 1 1⁄2 hours. Serve piping hot with Crubeens.

RED CABBAGE BAKE

SERVES 4

Ingredients:

- 1 small red cabbage, finely shredded
- 1/2 tablespoon salt
- 600 ml/1 pint/21/2 cups red wine
- 300 ml/1/2 pint/11/4 cups vegetable stock
- 150 ml/1/4 pint/2/3 cup wine vinegar
- 75 g/3 oz/1/3 cup caster (superfine) sugar
- 6 black peppercorns, crushed
- 1 teaspoon finely chopped fresh thyme
- 2 garlic cloves, finely chopped

Directions:

Sprinkle the cabbage with salt and leave to stand overnight until limp, then rinse and drain. Bring the wine, stock, vinegar and sugar to the boil in a saucepan. Add the peppercorns, thyme and garlic and return to the boil. Add the cabbage and boil for 2 minutes. Reduce the heat and simmer for 30 minutes. Serve hot as a vegetable, or cold with a salad.

HORSERADISH TERRINE

SERVES 4

Ingredients:

- 75 g/3 oz powdered gelatine
- 250 ml/8 fl oz/1 cup recently boiled water
- 2 tablespoons grated horseradish
- 1 teaspoon grated lemon rind
- 1/2 teaspoon lemon juice
- 1 teaspoon salt
- 4 drops of green food colouring
- 3 tablespoons double (heavy) cream

Directions:

Dissolve the gelatine in recently boiled water, then stir in the horseradish, lemon rind, juice and salt. Let the mixture cool slightly, then whisk in the colouring. Whip the cream until stiff, then fold into the mixture. Pour into a mould and leave to set. Chill before serving.

TOMATO SAUCE

SERVES 4

Ingredients:

- 50 g/2 oz/1⁄4 cup butter
- 1 bacon rasher (slice), rinded and chopped
- 1 onion, finely chopped
- 1 carrot, thinly sliced
- 450 g/1 lb ripe tomatoes, peeled and quartered
- 300 ml/1⁄2 pint/1 1⁄4 cups chicken stock
- 1 tablespoon plain (all-purpose) flour
- 3 tablespoons water
- 1 teaspoon caster (superfine) sugar
- 1⁄2 teaspoon lemon juice
- 1⁄4 teaspoon salt
- 1⁄4 teaspoon freshly ground black pepper

Directions:

Melt half the butter in a saucepan and sauté the bacon for 2 minutes, then add the onion and carrot and sauté for 5 minutes. Add the tomatoes, cover and cook for 5 minutes. Stir in the stock and bring to the boil. Mix the flour and water to a paste, then stir it into the pan with the sugar, lemon juice, salt and pepper. Cover and simmer for 30 minutes. Leave to cool, then rub through a sieve. Reheat the sauce and stir in the remaining butter.

Meat

———

Pork and ham figure substantially in Irish cookery, with Irish bacon forming an integral part of the Ulster fry, the day's first meal. In olden times, most homesteads had at least one pig, which would often live in the cottage itself. Anthony Trollope, the celebrated author who spent several years in Ireland, set his 1844 novel The Kellys and O'Kellys in the village of Dunmore in Connacht. He vividly describes the Irish country kitchen and its occupants: two pigs, a cockerel, three or four chickens, a dog and a heap of potatoes.

Pigs are so important a part of the Irish way of life that the first annual pig race, held in Naas in County Kildare, attracted a crowd of 7,000 spectators and speculators. Bookies donated their profits to charity, and the fastest trotters on the course belonged to a pig aptly named Porky's Revenge. Crubeens, a traditional Irish dish, is made from pigs' trotters, but hopefully not from a race competitor! Until quite recently, the traditional Irish peasant's cabin, or cottage, was a one-roomed, turf-thatched, stone-built structure. On the bleak west coast, these were sometimes set into the ground to offer more protection from the prevailing weather. Inside, the floor was of baked earth and the focal point was the turf fire. An iron pot, used for boiling potatoes, would stand on an iron griddle, used for cooking. A bed stood to the right of the fire, with four roof-high posts at each corner, to which straw mats were fitted for warmth and modesty. Other furniture consisted of four posts in the floor with wicker sides, serving as a potato bin, and deal shelves beside the bed, which were used as a dresser. There would be a few crude wooden stools and a chair made of straw. To one side of the door were pegs on which to hang cloaks, the main item of outdoor clothing, and above the door was a wicker-work hen-coop. This family home would usually be shared by a cow or one or more pigs, although one traveller in Ireland in 1837 remarked that he sometimes saw cabins so poor that there was not even one pig in them.

Turf fires are still common in the cottages out in the wilds of Ireland, and turf and peat cutters still operate, especially in the west of the country. Cutting turf for fuel is a time-consuming job. The turf is cut with a spade known as a *slane*, then spread out on a turf field. The process then involves footing, or stacking six turfs in a pyramid shape; rickling, or stacking the turfs on their sides; clamping, or stacking heaps of turfs near the access path; and finally, drawing them home to the cottage.

The field work, apart from the cutting, was usually done by women and children, and the drawing home was by the traditional Irish horse-drawn cart or *carr*. During the Iron Age, farmers fearing cattle rustlers on the shores of Lough Gara in Roscommon built artificial islands, or *crannogs,* in the lake. Around 300 of these islets exist, and dugout canoes were used to ferry the cattle over to the islets. *Crannogs* were in use up until the 1600s. In colloquial Gaelic, joints of meat were sometimes known as sproals, and small joints went by the name of *spoileens. Spoileens* was also the term used for travelling commercial kitchens. These were in the form of tents, in which two fires heated large pots of *spoileen*, a type of boiled mutton stew sold with bread. These spoileen tents would be found in fairgrounds and at any public celebrations, and were very popular across Ireland during the mid-nineteenth century. They were also probably a feature of Cork's famous Old English Market, which dates back to the late eighteenth century.

Mutton is the meat of a sheep over 18 months old; animals younger than that yield lamb. Some of the best lamb comes from the mountains and valleys where heather mingles with wild herbs, imparting a subtle hint of the moors and peat bogs and their wild flowers. Most mutton brought for the home table is between three and four years old. Mutton is very popular in Irish recipes and the local mutton is firm textured and close grained.

Salt-meadow mutton is favoured, the animals being raised on pastures rich in wild herbs, clover and shamrock. In the eighteenth century, some lamb recipes were most ambitious and often recommended seafood as an accompaniment. One popular stuffing for mutton and lamb consisted of oysters, crab meat and anchovies. Some early local recipes also suggested that carragheen, the Irish seaweed, went well with mutton.

Veal comes from two- to three-month-old calves which have been especially milk-fed. It is a tender, pink, firm flesh, and a noted delicacy. There are eight different cuts of veal, but the thin, tender escalopes, from the leg of the calf, are the most popular and the tastiest part of the animal. Probably the finest veal in Ireland comes from County Kerry, which is almost the only place you will find the native Kerry cattle. There is a proverb in both County Kerry and County Donegal which says: 'Kerry cows know Sunday.' This evolved from the tradition of taking blood from the cows to boil into a mixture with sorrel, making a wholesome broth for Sunday lunch when the peasant folk had no other food. The Irish are avid smokers of food – apart from the classic image of Irish pub-goers with clay pipes in their mouths! In many country cottages a smoked ham or two hangs from the beams. Smoke-houses exist all over Ireland. The Irish seem to smoke anything that runs, swims or flies, from beef and pork to pheasant and chicken, and from salmon, haddock and eel to trout, cod and herring. There are more than a dozen smoke-houses in Ireland which smoke ham in the traditional way.

Particularly popular in County Cork, drisheen is the name for a rich, dark blood sausage, or black pudding. A white variety is unique to

County Cork, where it is often served with tripe and can be made with lambs' blood. Commercially, drisheen is made by combining pigs' blood with finely minced pork fat trimmings, onions and herbs. Oatmeal or breadcrumbs are often added, and usually some cream and herbs such as mace or tansy. This mixture is then poured through a funnel into a length of pig's gut to form a long coil. The sausage is brushed with blood, which turns black when cooked, and boiled or poached until the blood sets. When drisheen is made at home, a shallow, wide pan is used in which to steam-bake the sausage in an oven.

CRUBEENS

SERVES 4

Ingredients:

- 4 pigs' trotters
- 1 onion, halved
- 1 carrot, quartered
- 6 peppercorns, crushed
- 1 bay leaf
- 1⁄2 tablespoon chopped fresh parsley
- 1 teaspoon chopped fresh thyme
- 1⁄4 teaspoon salt

Directions:

Place all the ingredients in a large pan and cover with cold water. Bring to the boil, then cover and simmer for 3 hours. Serve hot as a stew with Guinness and brown soda bread, or cold with salad.

TRADITIONAL ULSTER FRY

SERVES 4

Ingredients:

- 4 streaky bacon rashers (slices), rinded and chopped
- 6 eggs
- 2 tablespoons single (light) cream
- 1/2 teaspoon black pepper
- 25 g/1 oz/1/4 cup hard Irish cheese, grated
- 1 tablespoon chopped fresh chives

Directions:

Fry the bacon in a dry pan until crisp. Whisk the eggs in a bowl with the cream and pepper. Mix with the bacon and scramble over a gentle heat. Before it sets, add the cheese and chives and stir together.

ROAST HERB LAMB

SERVES 4–6

Ingredients:

- 1.5 kg/3 lb leg of lamb, trimmed
- 1 onion, chopped
- 150 ml/1⁄4 pint/2⁄3 cup water
- 3 tablespoons white wine
- salt and freshly ground black pepper

For the topping:

- 2 large garlic cloves
- 4 teaspoons grated root ginger
- grated rind of 1 lemon
- 2 tablespoons chopped
- fresh parsley
- 2 tablespoons chopped fresh mint
- 1 tablespoon chopped
- fresh rosemary
- 2 tablespoons olive oil

Directions:

Preheat the oven to 180°C/350°F/gas mark 4. Briefly blend the garlic, ginger, lemon rind, parsley, mint and rosemary to a fine mixture. Stir in the olive oil and blend to a paste. Place the joint in a roasting tin with the onion and water and cook in the oven for 45 minutes. Remove from the oven and spread the herb mixture over the joint. Return to the oven and cook for a further 30 minutes, topping up with water if necessary, until the lamb is cooked. Remove the meat from the pan and keep it warm. Discard the onion. Stir the wine into the pan juices, bring to the boil and simmer for a few minutes until reduced, stirring in all the cooking juices. Season with salt and pepper. Slice the lamb and serve with the gravy and Mint Sauce.

MINT SAUCE

SERVES 4

Ingredients:

- 2 tablespoons finely chopped fresh mint
- 2 teaspoons caster (superfine) sugar
- 1 tablespoon boiling water
- 4 tablespoons malt vinegar

Directions:

Pound the mint with the sugar in a mortar, then set aside for 30 minutes. Add the boiling water and stir until the sugar has dissolved, then stir in the vinegar.

MOUNTAIN MUTTON POT ROAST

SERVES 4–6

Ingredients:

- 1.5 kg/3 lb leg of mutton, boned
- 2 tablespoons corn oil
- 1 onion, sliced
- 2 celery sticks (stalks), sliced
- 4 carrots, halved
- 450 g/1 lb new potatoes
- 6 tablespoons mutton stock
- 1/4 teaspoon salt
- 1/4 teaspoon freshly ground black pepper

For the stuffing:

- 225 g/8 oz sausage meat
- 1 onion, chopped
- 1 tablespoon finely chopped fresh parsley
- 2 teaspoons dried oregano
- 1 garlic clove, crushed

Directions:

Preheat the oven to 160°C/325°F/gas mark 3. Mix together all the stuffing ingredients and use to stuff the mutton leg. Heat the oil in a flameproof casserole and brown the leg all over. Add the vegetables and stock and season with salt and pepper. Cover the casserole and cook in the oven for 2 hours until the mutton is tender. Slice the meat and serve with the vegetables.

STOUT BRAISED BEEF

SERVES 4

Ingredients:

- 3 tablespoons vegetable oil
- 3 onions, chopped
- 4 carrots, halved and sliced lengthways
- 3 tablespoons plain (all-purpose) flour
- salt and freshly ground black pepper
- 700 g/1½ lb beef steak, cut into 10 pieces
- 150 ml/¼ pint/⅔ cup Irish stout
- ½ teaspoon finely chopped fresh basil
- 150 ml/¼ pint/⅔ cup beef stock
- 1 teaspoon clear honey

Directions:

Preheat the oven to 190°C/375°F/gas mark 5. Heat the oil and sauté the onions until soft, then transfer to a casserole dish using a slotted spoon and add the carrots. Season the flour with salt and pepper and roll the beef in it. Brown the meat in the oil, then transfer to the casserole. Add the rest of the flour to the oil left in the pan and cook for 2 minutes, then stir in the stout and basil. Bring to the boil, then add the stock and honey. Stir well, then pour over the meat, cover the dish and cook in the oven for about 1½ hours until the meat is tender and the gravy has thickened. Serve with Horseradish Cream Sauce.

HORSERADISH CREAM SAUCE

SERVES 4

Ingredients:

- 3 tablespoons freshly grated horseradish
- 1 teaspoon mustard
- 1 teaspoon sugar
- 1 teaspoon lemon juice
- 1/2 teaspoon salt
- 1/4 teaspoon freshly ground black pepper
- 2 teaspoons vinegar
- 300 ml/1/2 pint/1 1/4 cups double (heavy) cream

Directions:

Mix together all the ingredients except the cream. Whip the cream until stiff, then fold it into the sauce and serve.

STEAK AND KIDNEY PUDDING

SERVES 4

Ingredients:

- 225 g/8 oz suet pastry
- 2 tablespoons plain (all-purpose) flour
- salt and freshly ground black pepper
- 350 g/12 oz stewing steak, cubed
- 100 g/4 oz kidney, trimmed and quartered
- 1 onion, finely chopped
- 3 tablespoons Irish stout

Directions:

Reserve a quarter of the pastry, then roll out the remainder on a lightly floured board and use to line a greased pudding bowl. Season the flour with salt and pepper, then coat the meat and kidneys in the flour, mix with the onion and put them into the basin. Pour in the stout. Roll out the reserved pastry to make a lid, dampen the edges with water and seal the pastry lid to the base. Cover with greaseproof paper and secure with string. Place the pudding in a large saucepan and fill with hot water to come half way up the sides of the basin. Cover and steam for 4 hours, topping up with boiling water as necessary, then serve piping hot.

KERRY KIDNEYS

SERVES 4

Ingredients:

- 50 g/2 oz/1⁄4 cup butter
- 2 onions, sliced
- 225 g/8 oz small sausages, halved
- 8 lambs' kidneys, cored, cleaned and halved
- 1 tablespoon plain (all-purpose) flour
- 300 ml/1⁄2 pint/1 1⁄4 cups stock
- 300 ml/1⁄2 pint/1 1⁄4 cups Irish stout
- 1 tablespoon tomato purée (paste)
- 1⁄4 teaspoon salt
- 1⁄4 teaspoon freshly ground black pepper
- 225 g/8 oz button mushrooms, sliced

Directions:

Preheat the oven to 160°C/325°F/gas mark 3. Melt the butter and sauté the onions until golden brown, then add the sausages and cook for 1 minute. Add the kidneys and sauté until browned, then turn all the ingredients into a casserole dish. Stir the flour into the butter remaining in the pan and cook over a low heat until brown, then add the stock, stout and tomato purée. Stir well and season with salt and pepper. Bring to the boil, then pour into the casserole. Cover and cook in the oven for 1 1⁄2 hours. Add the mushrooms, then return to the oven for 15 minutes until the meat is tender and the gravy is thick.

BACON AND POTATO SUPPER

SERVES 4

Ingredients:

- 450 g/1 lb pork sausages
- 8 thick back bacon rashers (slices), rinded
- 1.2 litres/2 pints/5 cups vegetable stock
- 8 potatoes, sliced
- 4 onions, sliced
- 3 tablespoons chopped fresh parsley
- 1⁄4 teaspoon salt
- 1⁄4 teaspoon freshly ground black pepper
- 2 teaspoons finely chopped chives

Directions:

Place the sausages, bacon and stock in a saucepan, bring to the boil, then simmer for 5 minutes. Add all the remaining ingredients except the chives, season with salt and pepper and return to the boil. Cover and simmer gently for 1 hour until the meat is cooked and the stew has thickened. Sprinkle the chives over the top and serve immediately.

TRADITIONAL BACON AND CABBAGE SUPPER

SERVES 4

Ingredients:

- 1 large Savoy cabbage, separated into leaves
- 10 bacon rashers (slices), rinded
- 5 allspice berries
- salt and freshly ground black pepper
- 300 ml/1⁄2 pint/1 1⁄4 cups ham stock

Directions:

Cook the cabbage in boiling salted water for 15 minutes. Drain, soak in cold water for 1 minute, then drain again and slice. Line an ovenproof dish with 5 bacon rashers, cover with the cabbage and sprinkle with allspice, salt and pepper. Lay the rest of the bacon on top and pour over the stock. Bring to the boil, cover and simmer for 1 hour until the stock has been absorbed. Serve hot.

HAM, PEA AND POTATO SUPPER

SERVES 4

Ingredients:

- 50 g/2 oz/1⁄4 cup butter
- 1 onion, chopped
- 600 ml/1 pint/21⁄2 cups ham stock
- 175 g/6 oz smoked ham, diced
- 100 g/4 oz peas
- 225 g/8 oz boiled potatoes, diced
- 4 tablespoons milk
- 1⁄2 teaspoon mustard
- 1⁄2 tablespoon cornflour (cornstarch)
- 1⁄4 teaspoon thyme
- 1⁄2 tablespoon finely chopped fresh parsley
- 1⁄4 teaspoon freshly ground black pepper

Directions:

Melt half the butter in a large saucepan and gently sauté the onion for 3 minutes. Add the stock, ham and peas. Bring up to a simmer and add the potatoes. Mix together the milk, mustard and cornflour into a paste, then stir it into the stew with the thyme and parsley. Simmer gently, without boiling, for 8 minutes. Season with the pepper, and stir in the rest of the butter. When the butter has melted, serve hot with soda bread.

GAMMON WITH WHISKEY SAUCE

SERVES 4

Ingredients:

- 4 gammon steaks, trimmed of fat
- 2 tablespoons unsalted (sweet) butter
- 1/2 tablespoon salted butter, softened
- 1/2 onion, finely chopped or grated
- 2 tablespoons plain (all-purpose) flour
- 175 ml/6 fl oz/3/4 cup vegetable stock
- 1 teaspoon soft brown sugar
- 2 teaspoons Irish whiskey
- salt and freshly ground black pepper

Directions:

Brush half the unsalted butter over one side of the steaks, then grill the steaks on the buttered side for 7 minutes. Turn the steaks, brush with the remaining butter and grill the other side. Meanwhile, heat the salted butter and sauté the onion until golden. Remove from the heat and stir in the flour, then blend in the stock. Return to the heat and add the sugar. Bring to the boil, stirring, then simmer for 2 minutes. Add the whiskey, salt and pepper and simmer until hot and well blended. Serve the gammon steaks with the sauce poured over them.

LIMERICK HAM

SERVES 8

Ingredients:

- 1 ham on the bone, cured and cooked
- 25 g/1 oz/1⁄4 cup juniper berries
- 250 ml/8 fl oz/1 cup gin
- 250 ml/8 fl oz/1 cup soft brown sugar
- 175 g/6 oz/2⁄3 cup coarse-grain mustard

Directions:

Preheat the oven to 200°C/400°F/gas mark 6. Deeply score the ham all over with a knife. Rub the juniper berries into the cuts, pushing them in. Mix together the gin, sugar and mustard. Cover the ham all over with the mixture. Place in an ovenproof dish and cover with baking foil. Bake in the oven for about 20 minutes until heated through. Remove the foil and bake for a further 20 minutes or so until the skin is crisp, basting regularly with the liquid produced.

DRISHEEN

SERVES 4

Ingredients:

- 1.2 litres/2 pints/5 cups sheep's blood (obtainable from some local butchers)
- 225 g/8 oz/2 cups oatmeal
- 2 teaspoons salt
- 600 ml/1 pint/2½ cups full cream milk
- 1 tablespoon single (light) cream
- ¼ teaspoon chopped fresh tansy
- ¼ teaspoon freshly ground black pepper

Directions:

Strain the blood into a bowl, and mix in all the remaining ingredients. Leave to stand for about an hour. Pour into a greased dish and cover with baking foil. Place in a large baking dish and pour enough boiling water around the dish to come half way up the sides. Bake in the oven at 160°C/325°F/gas mark 3 for about 30 minutes until set. Serve sliced.

GOOSEBERRY DRISHEEN SAUSAGES

SERVES 4

Ingredients:

- 225 g/8 oz drisheen or other
- black pudding, peeled and roughly chopped
- 6 spring onions (scallions), finely chopped
- 2 red (bell) peppers, seeded and diced
- 175 g/6 oz mashed potatoes
- 2 tablespoons mustard
- 2 tablespoons malt vinegar
- 1⁄4 teaspoon salt
- 1⁄4 teaspoon freshly ground black pepper
- 225 g/8 oz/2 cups plain (all-purpose) flour
- 4 eggs, lightly beaten
- 225 g/8 oz/4 cups fresh white breadcrumbs
- 3 tablespoons vegetable oil

For the compote:

- 350 g/12 oz/1 1⁄2 cups caster (superfine) sugar
- 600 ml/1 pint/2 1⁄2 cups water
- 225 g/8 oz gooseberries

Directions:

Blend the drisheen or black pudding, spring onions, peppers, potatoes, mustard, vinegar, salt and pepper in a food processor. Shape the mixture into little sausage shapes about 7.5 cm (3 inches) long. Roll them in the flour, then the eggs and then in the breadcrumbs. Heat the oil and sauté the sausages until golden brown. Drain and keep warm. To make the compote, dissolve the sugar in the water, bring to the boil and simmer for a few minutes to make a syrup. Add the gooseberries and cook for 10 minutes until soft. Strain off any excess juice and pour over the black pudding sausages to serve.

CABBAGE AND CORNED BEEF

SERVES 4

Ingredients:

- 900 g/2 lb corned beef brisket
- 1 onion
- 6 cloves
- 1 tablespoon chopped fresh parsley
- 1⁄2 teaspoon dried thyme
- 450 g/1 lb cabbage, coarsely shredded
- 4 potatoes, quartered
- 3 carrots, halved

For the sauce:

- 150 ml/1⁄4 pint/2⁄3 cup double (heavy) cream
- 1 tablespoon mayonnaise
- 3 tablespoons grated horseradish

Directions:

Place the meat in a saucepan, cover with water and bring to the boil. Press the cloves into the onion and add to the pan with the parsley and thyme and simmer for 1 hour. Skim the surface. Add the cabbage, potatoes and carrots. Simmer for about 25 minutes until the vegetables are cooked. Take off the heat, lift the meat out of the pan and cut it into chunks. Strain the vegetables and serve with the meat. To make the sauce, whip the cream until stiff, then fold in the mayonnaise and horseradish. Serve with the meat and vegetables.

HONEY-GLAZED HAM

SERVES 6–8

Ingredients:

- 1 x 1.5 kg/3 lb piece of smoked ham
- 1 large onion
- 8 cloves
- 6 peppercorns, crushed
- 3 tablespoons clear honey
- 2 tablespoons soft brown sugar
- 2 tablespoons vinegar

Directions:

Soak the ham in water overnight, then drain. Stud the onion with the cloves, place in a large saucepan with the ham and cover with water. Add the peppercorns and half the honey and bring to the boil. Skim off the scum, then simmer for about 1 hour and 20 minutes. Remove the ham from the pan and peel off the skin. Replace in the stock and allow to cool, then drain. Heat the sugar, vinegar and the remaining honey, stirring until mixed. Pour the mixture over the drained ham and leave to cool. Then serve thinly sliced.

SPICY ROAST PORK

SERVES 4–6

Ingredients:

- 1.5 kg/3 lb pork belly
- 2 tablespoons oil

For the stuffing:

- 75 g/3 oz/1⁄3 cup butter
- 1 onion, finely chopped
- 3 garlic cloves, crushed
- 225 g/8 oz/4 cups fine fresh breadcrumbs
- 1 teaspoon finely chopped mixed fresh herbs
- 1 egg, beaten
- 1⁄4 teaspoon salt
- 1⁄4 teaspoon freshly ground black pepper

For the paste:

- 2 tablespoons melted butter
- 2 tablespoons chutney
- 2 garlic cloves, crushed
- 1 tablespoon lemon juice
- 2 tablespoons mustard

Directions:

Preheat the oven to 180°/350°F/gas mark 4. To make the stuffing, heat the butter and sauté the onion and garlic until soft. Remove from the heat, stir in the breadcrumbs and herbs and leave to cool. Mix in the egg to bind the stuffing and season with salt and pepper. Mix together the paste ingredients. Prick the meat all over with a fork and rub half the paste all over the inside of the meat. Spread the stuffing over the meat, then roll it up with the stuffing inside and tie with string. Heat the oil in a roasting tin and brown the meat all over, then turn the meat seam-side up, transfer the pan to the oven and cook for 1 1⁄2 hours. Remove the meat from the oven, brush the outside with the rest of the paste and turn seam-side down. Return to the oven and cook for a further 1 1⁄2 hours. Serve sliced.

CLASSIC APPLE SAUCE

SERVES 4

Ingredients:

- 450 g/1 lb cooking (tart) apples,
- peeled, cored and sliced 4 cloves
- grated rind of 1⁄4 lemon
- 2 tablespoons caster (superfine) sugar
- 1 tablespoon butter

Directions:

Place the apples in a saucepan and rinse with water, then drain, leaving just the water clinging to the fruit. Add the cloves and lemon rind and cook gently for about 10 minutes until soft. Stir in the sugar and cook until dissolved. Rub the sauce through a sieve to make a purée. Stir in the butter and reheat gently to serve, or leave to cool.

Poultry and Game

In 1698, John Dunton, an English traveller in Ireland, recounted his experiences of staying with the Offlaghertie family. He was invited to walk a short distance to view their deer and was surprised to hear of a deer park in the wild place in which they were staying. However, after trekking through bogs and over mountains, the group came to Glinglass Vale, or the Green Valley, where they came across 'some hundreds of stately red deer, the stags bigger than a large English yearling calfe, with suitable antlers much bigger than I ever saw before.'

Dunton recounts it as the most pleasing scene he met with in the kingdom and after the group had retired for a vast beef and mutton dinner, 'myn host ordered his dogs to be gotten ready to hunt the stagg.'

HONEY-TRUSSED CHICKEN

SERVES 4

Ingredients:

- 1 x 1.5 kg/3 lb chicken
- 1 teaspoon coarse sea salt
- 1 lemon, halved
- 4 bay leaves, crushed
- 2 sprigs of fresh rosemary
- 3 tablespoons olive oil
- 2 tablespoons clear honey
- 1/4 teaspoon salt
- 1/4 teaspoon freshly ground black pepper
- 1 tablespoon chopped fresh parsley
- 1/2 tablespoon chopped fresh basil
- 1/2 tablespoon chopped fresh marjoram

Directions:

Preheat the oven to 200°C/400°F/gas mark 6. Rub the cavity of the chicken with the sea salt. Place half of the lemon inside the cavity, add the bay leaves and rosemary sprigs, then the second piece of lemon. Carefully tear back the skin from the top of the chicken breast. Mix together the olive oil and honey and season with salt and pepper. Rub half the mixture over the exposed breast. Mix together the parsley, basil and marjoram and sprinkle half the mixture over the top, then replace the skin over the breast. Slash the thighs three times on each side and rub the remaining herb mixture into the cuts. Rub the remaining honey and oil mixture over the chicken skin. Place the chicken, breast-side up in a baking dish. Cook in the oven for 10 minutes, then turn the chicken breast-side down and cook for 10 more minutes. Turn the chicken breast-side up and cook for about 1 hour until the juices run clear when pierced in the thickest part with a skewer.

WILD DUCK WITH BABY TURNIPS

SERVES 4

Ingredients:

- 4 bacon rashers (slices), rinded
- 1 celery stick (stalk), chopped
- 3 carrots, sliced
- 2 onions, sliced into rings
- 1 bay leaf
- 1 x 1.75 kg/4 lb oven-ready wild duck
- 300 ml/1⁄2 pint/1 1⁄4 cups dry cider
- 300 ml/1⁄2 pint/1 1⁄4 cups brown stock
- 24 whole baby turnips
- 1⁄4 teaspoon salt

Directions:

Arrange the bacon, celery, carrots, onions and bay leaf in a flameproof casserole dish and place the duck on top. Cook over a low heat for 10 minutes. Pour over the cider, bring to the boil and simmer until the cider has reduced by half. Pour over the stock, bring to the boil, cover and simmer very gently for 1 hour until the duck is tender. Meanwhile, cook the turnips in boiling salted water for 10 minutes. Remove the duck from the casserole and set aside. Skim off any fat from the surface of the dish, then rub the vegetables and liquid through a sieve to make a sauce and return it to the dish. Place the duck back in the dish and add the turnips. Heat through until the duck is very hot, then serve immediately.

GAELIC ROAST GOOSE

SERVES 8

Ingredients:

- 1 x 3.5 kg/8 lb oven-ready goose
- 25 g/1 oz/2 tablespoons butter
- 1 teaspoon salt
- 1/2 teaspoon freshly ground black pepper
- 1/4 teaspoon ground ginger
- 600 ml/1 pint/2 1/2 cups stock
- 150 ml/1/4 pint/2/3 cup port
- 1 lemon, quartered

For the stuffing:

- 2 onions, finely chopped
- 450 g/1 lb potatoes, boiled and mashed
- 225 g/8 oz sausage meat
- 120 ml/4 fl oz/1/2 cup double (heavy) cream
- 2 teaspoons dried sage
- 1/2 teaspoon salt
- 1/2 teaspoon freshly ground black pepper

Directions:

Preheat the oven to 180°C/350°F/gas mark 4. Mix together the stuffing ingredients and fill the goose. Truss the bird tightly, sewing each end. Mix the butter with the salt, pepper and ginger and spread this mixture over the breast. Place in a roasting tin and pour over the stock. Cook in the oven for 2 hours, pouring off excess fat from time to time. Stir the port into the cooking juices and return to the oven for a further 30 minutes until the goose is tender and the skin is crisp.

POT ROAST PHEASANT

SERVES 4

Ingredients:

- 2 tablespoons vegetable oil
- 1 tablespoon butter
- 1 large oven-ready pheasant
- 2 eating (dessert) apples, peeled, cored and quartered
- 1 onion, chopped
- 4 teaspoons plain (all-purpose) flour
- 150 ml/1/4 pint/2/3 cup stock
- 150 ml/1/4 pint/2/3 cup red wine
- 1 tablespoon soft brown sugar
- juice of 1 orange
- 1/4 teaspoon salt
- 1/4 teaspoon freshly ground black pepper
- 1 bay leaf
- 1 sprig of fresh thyme
- 1 sprig of fresh savory
- 2 sprigs of fresh parsley

Directions:

Preheat the oven to 150°C/300°F/gas mark 2. Heat the oil and butter in a frying pan and brown the pheasant on all sides. Transfer the pheasant to a casserole dish and add the apple quarters. Add the onion to the pan and sauté until soft. Stir in the flour and cook for 1 minute, then add the stock, wine, sugar and orange juice and bring to the boil, stirring until smooth. Season with salt and pepper and pour over the pheasant. Tie the herbs into a bundle and add to the dish.

Cover the casserole and cook in the oven for 1 hour until the juices run clear when you pierce the thickest part of the meat with a skewer. Discard the herbs before serving.

PEASANT'S PARTRIDGE POT

SERVES 4

Ingredients:

- 225 g/8 oz shallots
- 100 g/4 oz streaky bacon, rinded and diced
- 2 oven-ready partridges
- 225 g/8 oz button mushrooms, stalks removed
- 600 ml/1 pint/2½ cups stock
- ¼ tablespoon finely chopped fresh lovage
- 225 g/8 oz/1 cup butter
- 1 tablespoon plain (all-purpose) flour
- juice of ½ lemon
- salt and freshly ground black pepper

Directions:

Preheat the oven to 150°C/300°F/gas mark 2. Finely chop and reserve two of the shallots. Cook half the bacon in a flameproof casserole dish until the fat runs, then add the partridges and cook until browned all over. Add the whole shallots and the mushroom caps. Pour in half the stock, add the lovage, cover and transfer to the oven for 2 hours.

Meanwhile, heat the butter and sauté the rest of the bacon and the chopped shallots until browned. Add the mushroom stalks, stir in the flour and cook for 1 minute, stirring. Whisk in the remaining stock, bring to the boil and simmer until thick. Stir in the lemon juice and season with salt and pepper. Lift the partridge and vegetables from the casserole and arrange on a serving dish. Discard any fat and keep warm. Stir a little of the cooking juices from the partridge into the sauce until it is the consistency you prefer. Pour over the partridges to serve.

HOMESTEAD RABBIT PIE

SERVES 4

Ingredients:

- 50 g/2 oz/1⁄4 cup butter
- 4 rabbit portions
- 1 onion, chopped
- 50 g/2 oz bacon, rinded and chopped
- 175 g/6 oz mushrooms, sliced
- 150 ml/1⁄4 pint/2⁄3 cup Irish stout
- 150 ml/1⁄4 pint/2⁄3 cup chicken stock
- 2 tablespoons cornflour (cornstarch)
- 1⁄4 teaspoon salt
- 1⁄4 teaspoon freshly ground black pepper
- 175 g/6 oz puff pastry
- 1 tablespoon milk

Directions:

Preheat the oven to 200°C/400°F/gas mark 6. Melt half the butter and sauté the rabbit portions until browned on all sides, then remove from the pan. Add the onion, bacon and mushrooms to the pan and fry until softened, then return the rabbit to the pan and pour over the stout. Bring to the boil, cover and simmer for about 15 minutes. Blend the stock with the cornflour, salt and pepper, stir into the pan and simmer, stirring until thickened. Continue to cook for a further 15 minutes until the rabbit is tender. Spoon into a greased ovenproof dish. Roll out the pastry on a lightly floured board and press over the dish, sealing the edges and decorating with the pastry trimmings. Make a hole in the

centre of the pastry for steam to escape and brush the top
with the milk. Bake in the oven for about 20 minutes until
the pastry is golden brown.

POACHER'S JUGGED WILD HARE

SERVES 4

Ingredients:

- 1 hare, jointed
- 900 ml/1 1⁄2 pints/3 3⁄4 cups Irish stout
- 6 peppercorns, crushed
- 1 bay leaf
- 2 tablespoons corn oil
- 50 g/2 oz/1⁄4 cup butter
- 3 streaky bacon rashers (slices), rinded
- 450 g/1 lb small onions, roughly chopped
- 1 garlic clove crushed with
- 1 teaspoon salt
- 1⁄2 tablespoon plain (all-purpose) flour
- 1⁄2 teaspoon dried basil
- 1⁄2 teaspoon dried oregano
- 3 tablespoons chicken stock
- 25 g/1 oz/2 tablespoons margarine
- 225 g/8 oz button mushrooms

Directions:

Place the hare in a dish, pour over the stout and add the peppercorns, bay leaf and oil. Cover and leave to stand in a cool place overnight. Remove from the marinade and pat dry on kitchen paper. Heat the butter in a large saucepan and sauté the bacon for 3 minutes. Add the hare and sauté until browned, then remove from the pan. Add half the onions and the crushed garlic and sauté until softened, then return the hare to the pan. Sprinkle with the flour, basil and oregano and cook for 1 minute. Strain in the marinade, add the stock and bring to the boil. Cover and simmer for 3 hours until the hare is very tender, adding a little more stout or stock if necessary during cooking. Heat the margarine and lightly sauté the remaining onions and the mushrooms until just golden. Remove the hare from the pan and keep warm. Add the fried onions and mushrooms to the sauce and heat, uncovered, for a few minutes until reduced and thickened, then pour over the hare to serve.

WHISKEY-GRILLED WILD BOAR STEAKS

SERVES 4

Ingredients:

- 6 juniper berries, crushed
- 2 tablespoons vegetable oil
- 1 tablespoon clear honey
- 1 tablespoon Irish whiskey
- 1/2 teaspoon paprika
- 1/4 teaspoon salt
- 1/4 teaspoon freshly ground black pepper
- 4 x 225 g/8 oz wild boar steaks
- 4 sprigs of fresh rosemary

Directions:

Mix together the juniper berries, oil, honey, whiskey, paprika, salt and pepper. Brush the steaks on both sides with the mixture. Place one steak on a large piece of baking foil and pile the rest of the steaks on top of each other. Pour any excess marinade over the steaks and wrap the foil around the steaks. Leave to marinate in a refrigerator for at least 3 hours. Remove the steaks from the marinade and place on an oiled grill. Cook for about 6 minutes each side, spooning over any excess marinade as they cook. Serve garnished with the rosemary sprigs.

FLUMMOXED VENISON

SERVES 4

Ingredients:

- 900 g/2 lb venison, cubed
- 450 ml/3⁄4 pint/2 cups mead or red wine
- 2 bay leaves
- 1 bouquet garni
- 25 g/1 oz/1⁄4 cup plain (all-purpose) flour
- 50 g/2 oz/1⁄4 cup butter
- 2 onions, chopped
- 2 carrots, chopped
- 150 ml/1⁄4 pint/2⁄3 cup Irish stout
- 25 g/1 oz/1⁄4 cup cornflour (cornstarch)
- 1⁄4 teaspoon salt
- 1⁄4 teaspoon freshly ground black pepper

Directions:

Place the venison in a glass or ceramic bowl, pour over the mead or wine, add the bay leaves and bouquet garni, cover and leave to marinate overnight. Remove the meat from the marinade and pat dry on kitchen paper. Roll the meat in the flour, shaking off any excess. Heat the butter in a large saucepan and sauté the meat until browned on all sides. Strain the marinade over the meat and add the onions and carrots. Bring to the boil, then cover and simmer for about 11⁄2 hours until tender. Blend the stout with the cornflour, stir into the saucepan and bring to the boil. Season with salt and pepper and simmer for 2 minutes, stirring until the sauce thickens, then serve hot.

CLASSIC BROWN SAUCE FOR MEAT OR VENISON

SERVES 4

Ingredients:

- 2 tablespoons beef dripping
- 1 onion, chopped
- 1 carrot, thinly sliced
- 2 bacon rashers (slices), rinded and chopped
- 25 g/1 oz/1⁄4 cup plain (all-purpose) flour
- 450 ml/3⁄4 pint/2 cups stock
- 2 tablespoons port or red wine
- 1 teaspoon tomato purée (paste)
- 1⁄4 teaspoon salt
- 1⁄4 teaspoon freshly ground black pepper

Directions:

Heat the dripping and sauté the onion, carrot and bacon until brown. Stir in the flour and cook gently for 15 minutes. Slowly add the stock, stirring well until smooth. Add the port or wine and tomato purée, and season with salt and pepper. Bring to the boil and simmer for 30 minutes. Rub the sauce through a sieve before serving.

BREAD SAUCE

SERVES 4

Ingredients:

- 300 ml/1⁄2 pint/1 1⁄4 cups milk
- 1 onion, quartered
- 1 bay leaf
- 50 g/2 oz/1 cup fresh white breadcrumbs
- 1 tablespoon butter
- 1 tablespoon single (light) cream
- salt and freshly ground black pepper

Directions:

Place the milk in a saucepan with the onion and bay leaf and bring almost to the boil. Remove from the heat, cover and set aside for 30 minutes. Strain into a clean pan and stir in the breadcrumbs, butter and cream, then season to taste with salt and pepper.

Desserts and Drinks

Ireland's brewing industry has a long history going back to medieval times. During the 1200s, the waters of the Poddle River in Dublin provided the first of the raw materials for ale brewing, and local ale fast became the island's national drink. By the mid-1660s Dublin was the centre of the Irish ale business and there were more than 90 brew pubs and almost 2,000 ale houses in a city of only 4,000 families. As early as 1670, Giles Mee was brewing an ordinary ale on a site near Dublin city's old entrance, St James's Gate. Then in about 1693, the brewing rights were transferred to Sir Mark Rainsford, and the business remained in that family until the brewery was leased to a John Paul Espinasse in 1715. On his death in 1750, the brewery went into disuse for a decade.

During the mid-eighteenth century in London, an ale made popular by the fruit and vegetable porters of Covent Garden, and those working in Billingsgate fish market, became known as porter. The addition of roasted barley to the ale gave the drink a distinctive dark colour and a slightly malty taste. In Dublin in 1759, a 34-year-old Irishman named Arthur Guinness decided that the English were not the only ones who could brew a fine porter, and approached the owner of the derelict St James's Brewery.

With true Irish optimism, Guinness signed a 9,000-year lease on the brewery, agreeing to a £45-a-year rent. To see this lease out, Arthur Guinness would have to live until he was 9,034 years of age, beating Methuselah by 8,065 years!

However, he began his business by first brewing a traditional Dublin ale, and later developing a strong porter which he called Extra Stout

Porter, later shortened to stout, or Guinness stout. The popularity of his new brew overtook that of the local ale and it was soon being transported around Ireland through the newly constructed canal network. In 1803, Arthur Guinness passed away at the ripe old age of 78, handing the business over to his son, also named Arthur. By the early part of the nineteenth century, the Guinness brewery was producing 66,000 barrels of stout a year, but the largest brewery was, in fact, Beamish and Crawford of Cork, which produced 100,000 barrels.

By 1833, however, Guinness had become the largest brewery in Ireland and, by the time of Arthur Guinness II's death in 1855, had become the largest brewery in the world. The brewery was revamped in 1886 and even contained its own railway!

Guinness very quickly developed a strong export trade and even under the first Arthur Guinness, Guinness West Indies Porter was being shipped to the Caribbean. Guinness Strong Foreign Extra Stout (FES), with its 7.5 per cent alcohol content, was brewed in much the same way. This was developed by Arthur Guinness II especially for the export trade. The stout is matured for three months in wooden barrels, then blended with a young stout. So popular was the Guinness stout in England that a branch of the brewery was opened in Park Royal in London in 1936. Guinness went on to establish more breweries abroad, including Nigeria, Malaysia, Cameroon, Jamaica and Ghana. Guinness is now brewed in more than 45 different countries in all five continents and sold in 55 countries.

Guinness stout is made entirely with Irish products: 90,000 tons of home-grown barley are used each year, as are local hops, yeast and Ireland's famous water. The brewery stands near the banks of Dublin's River Liffey, although the water used for brewing comes from the Wicklow Mountains. Guinness begins as a sweet liquid known as 'wort', made by straining a 'mash' made from roasted and milled barley and water through a device known as a 'kieve'. Hops are added to the wort before it is boiled in huge coppers for one and a half hours, when the wort is left to settle for around 40 minutes, then left to cool. Yeast is then added to start the fermentation process, converting the nutrients and sugars in the wort into alcohol. An unfermented wort, known as 'gyle', is then added to the beer, which undergoes a second fermentation and is left to mature. The beer is clarified and, most importantly, tasted before distribution.

The final product itself, the celebrated Irish stout – known variously as the wine of the country, the icon of Irishness, the dark stuff, the parish priest or the blonde in the black skirt – is the ideal accompaniment to Ireland's traditional fare, especially cheese, meat dishes and seafood, which is why it is often called the essence of good living. The Guinness brewery not only produces the famous draught and bottled stout, however – it also produces beers, lager and cider. Cider is one of the first alcoholic beverages ever to be fermented. It is thought that the art of cider-making in Ireland originated with the advent of the Vikings, and the drink quickly became more popular than the local mead. Today's Irish cider can vary from two to eight per cent alcohol. Whilst Guinness is the beer of 'Dublin's fair city', Cork also has two major breweries: Murphy's and Beamish. The country's second largest brewers, James J. Murphy was established at Lady's Well in Cork in 1856.

Murphy's began by brewing porter, but switched to stout as its popularity grew. Lane's Southgate Brewery was established in Cork in 1758, and was then taken over by Beamish and Crawford, which was initially the Cork Porter Brewery, founded in 1792. There are also several breweries in Ulster, including the Herald brewery at Lisburn and Hilden's brewery in Coleraine. A newcomer to the Irish stout scene is Caffrey's, and there are several other independent breweries, such as Smithwicks and Whitewater, which brew ales, stout and porter.

Nothing is wasted in the process of brewing stout, as all the by-products go back to the land. Farmers use as animal feed the 'screenings', or barley too small for brewing; the 'combings', or little roots grown by the partially germinated barley; the 'trub', the waste produced after yeast is added to the wort; and any surplus yeast.

One famous stout drink that is distinctly un-Irish is Black Velvet. Black Velvet is made with equal quantities of iced stout and champagne, poured into a glass simultaneously but not stirred, and drunk whilst the bubbles remain. 'There's more friendship in a glass of whiskey than in a barrel of buttermilk' is an old Irish saying, and as far back as the sixteenth century, Queen Elizabeth I once commented that Irish whiskey was her only true Irish friend – although this may have had more to do with the politics of the day than her real opinion of the whiskey!

Irish whiskey has been distilled from a base of barley and malted barley in Ireland for centuries, and records of whiskey distilling date back to the sixth century. The whiskey is made with barley dried on a solid floor over fires, which prevents the smoke from permeating the barley. For Scotch whisky, on the other hand, the grain is dried over peat fires, imparting a different flavour to the grain. The Irish method ensures a smoothness which peat-fire heat cannot attain. Most Irish whiskey is pot stilled three times and matured for around five years before reaching the market.

The oldest commercial whiskey distillery in the world is Bushmills in Cork on the banks of the River Bush, and the company was licensed to distil whiskey in 1608. Other well-known distillers are Powers in Dublin, and the Jamieson label, with numerous ages and types of whiskey, from County Antrim. There is also the Paddy range of whiskies, and Redbreast, Green Spot and Tullamore Dew. Less well known are the whiskeys of the Cooley distillery on the Cooley peninsula near Dundalk in County Louth, in the east of Ireland, which are aged in the original Locke's Distillery in Kilbeggan, County Westmeath. These include Connemara, a single malt which has a local, peaty flavour similar to the blended Irish Inishowen; the Derry single malt known as Tyrconnell with its oily, woody flavour; the excellent light whiskey named Millar's after an old Dublin tipple; and Kilbeggan with its delightful aroma.

Drinking toasts is a common Irish custom, and in the early days, the peasant's drinking vessel was a wooden mug, or madder. However, in the grand country houses, some drinking glasses were long and thin without a base, so the drinker would have to drink the entire contents before replacing it on the table. More than a few toasts with this form of drinking glass would be unwise! As in every country in the world, the Irish have their form of 'Cheers': a toast is drunk with the word 'Slainte!' or 'good health'. One landlord famous for his toasts and drinking songs was John O'Toumy, who presided over a popular inn in Mungret Street, Limerick, in the 1700s. The inn served as a meeting place for poets and many a bard learned his art at O'Toumy's bar.

Most people have heard of the clandestine distilling of an alcoholic spirit in Ireland, known as poteen, or poitin, which means 'little pot still'. With possibly more names than the number of accounts of sightings of the little people, poteen is variously known as holy water, mountain dew, water of life, or a string of other euphemisms. Originally thought to date back to the sixth century, distilling poteen became widespread many years ago when the tax on whiskey became unacceptably high, and each distiller would create their own unique recipe, usually involving potatoes and grain. This home-brewed spirit has been illegal in Ireland since 1661, under King Charles II's laws, but today a commercially made poteen is available.

In one of the traditional recipes, the usquebagh begins as a wash of grapes, raisins, black treacle, sugar and yeast in water, which is left to ferment for three weeks. The wash is strained into a boiler, in which it is heated to boiling point and begins to give off steam. The steam is channelled into a long, spiral, copper pipe, known as the worm, which runs down into a barrel filled with cold water. When the hot steam cools, it condenses in the tube and can be tapped off as a clear, 140-degree-proof poteen – much too powerful to drink! After the first quantity has been bled off, the tipple becomes weaker and more palatable. The run, as it is called, takes around three hours from boiling to bottling. The poteen is then tested for strength and taste. Its alcoholic purity is tested by dipping a twist of paper in the brew, then lighting it.

The blue flame should not consume the paper. A finger is subjected to the same treatment and the tester should remain unscathed by the ordeal. The third, and best, test is to sample the poteen by drinking it!

TIPSY PUDDING

SERVES 4

Ingredients:

- For the pudding
- 75 g/3 oz/1⁄3 cup caster (superfine) sugar
- 3 eggs
- 75 g/3 oz/3⁄4 cup plain (all-purpose) flour
- 1⁄2 teaspoon vanilla essence (extract)
- 2 tablespoons cornflour (cornstarch)
- 225 g/8 oz/2⁄3 cup fruit jam (conserve)
- 120 ml/4 fl oz/1⁄2 cup Irish whiskey
- 5 tablespoons sherry

For the topping

- 2 egg yolks
- 1 teaspoon cornflour (cornstarch)
- 1 tablespoon granulated sugar
- 1⁄4 teaspoon vanilla essence (extract)
- 300 ml/1⁄2 pint/1 1⁄4 cups milk
- 300 ml/1⁄2 pint/1 1⁄4 cups double (heavy) cream
- 50 g/2 oz/1⁄2 cup almonds, toasted

Directions:

Preheat the oven to 200°C/400°F/gas mark 6 and line a wide, flat baking sheet with oiled baking foil. Whisk together the sugar and eggs in a bowl over a pan of hot water until pale. Fold in the flour and vanilla essence, then pour the batter into the baking sheet. Bake in the oven for about 8 minutes until springy to the touch. Turn out on to a cornflour-dusted surface and remove the foil. Spread the jam over the surface of the cake and roll up from the long side. Set on dish to cool, then pour the whiskey and sherry over the top. To make the topping, whisk the egg yolks, cornflour, sugar and vanilla essence into the milk in a bowl set over a pan of simmering water. Stir over a low heat until the mixture is thick, then pour over the roll, leave to cool and refrigerate for 1 hour. Whip the cream until stiff, then spread over pudding and decorate with toasted almonds.

ORCHARD APPLES IN WHISKEY SAUCE

SERVES 4

Ingredients:

- 4 red eating (dessert) apples
- 4 green eating (dessert) apples
- 50 g/2 oz/1/4 cup butter
- 1 cinnamon stick
- 10 cloves
- 50 g/2 oz/1/4 cup caster (superfine) sugar
- 4 teaspoons clear honey

For the sauce:

- 6 egg yolks
- 75 g/3 oz/1/3 cup caster (superfine) sugar
- 6 tablespoons Irish whiskey

Directions:

Poach the red apples in a saucepan of simmering water for 6 minutes. Remove and leave to cool. Make the sauce by whisking the egg yolks, sugar and whiskey in a bowl set over a pan of simmering water until pale and thick. (Do not overheat or the sauce will curdle.) Remove from the heat and keep warm. Slice off and keep the tops of the red apples, then carefully scoop out and chop the flesh. Discard the core. Peel, quarter and core the green apples and cut into segments. Melt the butter and sauté the apple segments with the cinnamon, cloves, sugar and honey until the apples are cooked. Discard the spices and simmer to reduce the remaining liquid. Arrange the red apple flesh in the bottom of their hollowed-out skins and arrange the segments on top. Place the apples in the centre of warm plates, then pour the sauce from the pan around the edges. Spoon the whiskey sauce over the top of the apples, replace the tops and serve.

CARRAGHEEN COCOA DESSERT

SERVES 4

Ingredients:

- 2 large handfuls of dried carragheen
- 900 ml/1 1⁄2 pints/3¾ cups milk
- 300 ml/1⁄2 pint/1 1⁄4 cups water
- 4 tablespoons cocoa (unsweetened chocolate) powder
- 3 tablespoons caster (superfine) sugar
- 2 drops of vanilla essence (extract)
- 300 ml/1⁄2 pint/1 1⁄4 cups double (heavy) cream, whipped

Directions:

Soak the carragheen in cold water for 2 hours, then drain. Bring milk and water to the boil, then add the carragheen and simmer for 1 hour. Purée in a food processor or blender. Mix the cocoa, sugar and vanilla essence with a little milk, add this paste to the carragheen mixture and stir well. Chill, then serve with the whipped cream.

YALLER SPOTTED DOG

SERVES 4

Ingredients:

- 225 g/8 oz/2 cups plain (all-purpose) flour
- 225 g/8 oz/2 cups corn meal
- 1 teaspoon caster (superfine) sugar
- 1 teaspoon salt
- 1 teaspoon bicarbonate of soda (baking soda)
- 5 tablespoons buttermilk
- 100 g/4 oz/2⁄3 cup sultanas (golden raisins)
- 1 tablespoon milk

Directions:

Preheat the oven to 180°C/350°F/gas mark 4. Sift the flour, corn meal, sugar, salt and bicarbonate of soda into a bowl, then stir in the buttermilk until the mixture becomes tacky. Turn out on to a floured board and knead in the sultanas. Shape into a round, flat cake, cut a cross on the top and brush with the milk. Bake in the oven for about 45 minutes until the cake sounds hollow when tapped on the base. Serve warm with lots of butter.

STOUT CISTE

SERVES 4

Ingredients:

- 300 ml/1⁄2 pint/1 1⁄4 cups stout
- 225 g/8 oz/1 cup soft brown sugar
- 225 g/8 oz/1 cup butter
- 225 g/8 oz/1 1⁄3 cups raisins
- 225 g/8 oz/1 1⁄3 cups sultanas (golden raisins)
- 225 g/8 oz/1 1⁄3 cups currants
- 50 g/2 oz/1⁄4 cup glacé (candied) cherries, quartered
- 550 g/1 1⁄4 lb/5 cups plain (all-purpose) flour
- 1 teaspoon ground allspice
- 1⁄2 teaspoon bicarbonate of soda (baking soda)
- 3 eggs, beaten

Directions:

Preheat the oven to 160°C/325°F/gas mark 3. Place the stout, sugar and butter in a pan over a low heat and stir until the butter melts. Mix in the fruit, bring to the boil and simmer for 4 minutes. Remove from the heat and leave to cool. Mix the flour, allspice and soda in a bowl, then stir in the fruit mixture and the eggs. Turn into a greased and lined 20 cm (8 inch) cake tin. Bake in the oven for 2 hours until a knife inserted in the centre comes out clean. Leave to cool in the tin before turning out.

SWEET HONEYED OATS

SERVES 4

Ingredients:

- 300 ml/1⁄2 pint/1 1⁄4 cups milk
- 175 g/6 oz/1 1⁄2 cups rolled oats
- 50 g/2 oz/1⁄4 cup caster (superfine) sugar
- 2 tablespoons Irish heather honey
- 25 g/1 oz/2 tablespoons butter
- 1⁄2 teaspoon ground cinnamon
- 1⁄2 teaspoon allspice
- finely grated rind of 1 orange
- 3 eggs, separated

Directions:

Bring the milk to the boil in a saucepan. Sprinkle in the oats and simmer gently for 5 minutes, stirring. Beat in the sugar, honey, butter, spices and orange rind. Remove from the heat and leave to cool slightly, then beat in the egg yolks. Whisk the egg whites until stiff, then carefully fold them into the mixture. Turn into a greased pudding basin, cover with pleated greaseproof paper and place in a large saucepan. Fill the saucepan with boiling water to come half way up the sides of the basin, cover and steam for 2 hours, topping up with boiling water as necessary. Turn on to a dish and serve with fragrant honey and cream.

CRANACHAN

SERVES 4

Ingredients:

- 350 ml/12 fl oz/1⅓ cups double (heavy) cream
- 4 tablespoons clear honey
- 4 tablespoons Irish whiskey
- 75 g/3 oz/¾ cup rolled oats, toasted
- 50 g/2 oz/½ cup ground almonds, toasted
- 1 teaspoon lemon juice
- 1 orange, sliced

Directions:

Whip the cream until stiff, then fold in the honey and whiskey. Stir in the rolled oats and almonds, then the lemon juice. Chill, then serve garnished with orange slices.

HEATHER HONEY MOUSSE

SERVES 4

Ingredients:

- 4 large eggs, separated
- 450 g/1 lb/1 1/3 cups clear
- heather honey

Directions:

Mix the egg yolks with the honey in a bowl set over a pan of gently simmering water. Keep stirring until the mixture forms a custard. Remove the pan from the heat and leave to cool. Whisk the egg whites until they stand up in peaks, then gently fold into the cool mixture. Spoon into individual dishes and chill for 3–4 hours before serving.

BROSE

SERVES 4

Ingredients:

- 3 tablespoons rolled oats
- 300 ml/1⁄2 pint/1 1⁄4 cups double (heavy) cream
- 1 tablespoon clear honey
- 2 tablespoons Irish whiskey

Directions:

Soak the oats in boiling water for 1 hour, then pour into a sieve. Press with the back of a spoon until most of the water is expelled. Whip the cream until stiff, then fold in the honey and whiskey. Stir in the oats and serve.

RUSTIC RHUBARB TART

SERVES 4

Ingredients:

- 350 g/12 oz puff pastry
- 450 g/1 lb rhubarb, sliced
- 175 g/6 oz/3⁄4 cup butter, melted
- 175 g/6 oz/3⁄4 cup soft brown sugar
- 300 ml/1⁄2 pint/1 1⁄4 cups double (heavy) cream
- 100 g/4 oz/1⁄2 cup caster (superfine) sugar
- 2 teaspoons Irish whiskey
- 4 sprigs of fresh mint

Directions:

Preheat oven to 180°C/350°F/gas mark 4. Roll out the pastry on a lightly floured board, cut into four equal circles and turn up the edges of each one to make tart cases and place on a greased baking sheet. Divide the rhubarb equally between the tarts, then brush with the melted butter and sprinkle with the brown sugar. Cook in the oven for 30 minutes until the rhubarb is tender and the sugar has caramelized on top. Make the sauce by whipping the cream until stiff, then whisking in the caster sugar and whiskey. Serve the tarts with the whiskey cream and garnish with the sprigs of mint.

BRUIDEN TART

SERVES 4

Ingredients:

- 225 g/8 oz shortcrust pastry
- 50 g/2 oz/1⁄2 cup ground almonds
- 4 large cooking (tart) apples, peeled, cored and sliced
- 2 tablespoons granulated sugar
- 3 egg yolks, beaten
- 50 g/2 oz/1⁄4 cup caster (superfine) sugar
- 300 ml/1⁄2 pint/1 1⁄4 cups double (heavy) cream
- 2 teaspoons Irish whiskey

Directions:

Preheat oven to 180°C/350°F/gas mark 4. Roll out the pastry on a lightly floured board and use to line four greased pie tins. Sprinkle the ground almonds over the pastry cases, place the apple slices on top and sprinkle with granulated sugar. Beat the egg yolks and caster sugar until pale and fluffy. Warm the cream slightly, then stir it into the egg and sugar mixture. Stir in the whiskey. Spoon a little of the cream mixture into each tart to cover the apples and reserve the remaining cream. Bake the tarts in the oven for 25–35 minutes until golden on top. Meanwhile, heat the remaining cream in a bowl set over a pan of gently simmering water and stir until it thickens, then serve with the tarts.

WHISKEY CHOCOLATE CAKE

MAKES one 20 cm (8 inch) cake

Ingredients:

- 2 eggs
- 75 g/3 oz/⅓ cup caster (superfine) sugar
- 50 g/2 oz/¼ cup butter
- 100 g/4 oz plain (semi-sweet) chocolate
- 50 g/2 oz/½ cup crushed hazelnuts
- 250 ml/8 fl oz/1 cup Irish whiskey
- 225 g/8 oz digestive biscuits (Graham crackers), crushed
- 3 tablespoons double (heavy) cream
- 50 g/2 oz/½ cup whole hazelnuts
- 50 g/2 oz/¼ cup glacé (candied) cherries

Directions:

Whisk together the eggs and sugar until pale. Melt the butter and chocolate in a pan, then fold in the egg mixture. Stir in the crushed hazelnuts and half the whiskey. Sprinkle the crushed biscuits into a greased and lined 20 cm (8 inch) cake tin. Pour the chocolate mixture into the tin and place in a refrigerator overnight. Whip the cream until stiff, then fold in the remaining whiskey. Turn out the cake, pipe the cream on the top and decorate with whole hazelnuts and glacé cherries.

AISLING APPLE CAKE

SERVES 4

Ingredients:

- 100 g/4 oz/1⁄2 cup butter
- 225 g/8 oz/2 cups plain (all-purpose) flour
- 1⁄2 teaspoon baking powder
- 100 g/4 oz/1⁄2 cup granulated sugar
- 1 egg, lightly beaten
- 3 tablespoons milk
- 2 cooking (tart) apples, peeled,
- cored and chopped
- 2 tablespoons soft brown sugar
- 3 cloves

Directions:

Preheat the oven to 200°C/400°F/gas mark 6. Rub the butter into the flour and baking powder. Stir in the sugar, then add the egg and enough of the milk to make a dough. Roll out half the dough and use to line a greased pie dish. Arrange the apples on the pastry, sprinkle with brown sugar and add the cloves. Roll out the remaining dough, cover the pie and seal the edges with a little milk. Cook in the oven for 40 minutes until browned.

MACHA'S COFFEE MERINGUE

MAKES one 20 cm (8 inch) cake

Ingredients:

- 3 egg whites
- 75 g/3 oz/1/3 cup caster (superfine) sugar
- 75 g/3 oz/1/2 cup icing (confectioners') sugar
- 1 1/2 tablespoons instant coffee
- 450 ml/3/4 pint/2 cups double (heavy) cream
- 2 tablespoons Irish whiskey

Directions:

Preheat the oven to 120°C/250°F/gas mark 1. Whisk egg whites until stiff. Beat in the caster sugar. Sift the icing sugar and mix it with the coffee, then fold into the egg mixture. Spread the mixture into two 20 cm (8 inch) circles on a lined baking sheet and cook in the oven for 4 hours until hard and dry on the outside, but soft inside. Whip the cream until stiff, then stir in the whiskey. Spread the cream on the flat side of one meringue round and place the second meringue on top.

JAMIESON'S CAKE

MAKES one 20 cm (8 inch) cake

Ingredients:

- 350 g/12 oz/2 cups mixed dried fruit
- 75 g/3 oz/1⁄3 cup glacé (candied) cherries
- 120 ml/4 fl oz/1⁄2 cup Jamieson's or other Irish whiskey
- 175 g/6 oz/2⁄3 cup butter
- 175 g/6 oz/2⁄3 cup soft brown sugar
- 4 eggs, beaten
- a few drops of vanilla essence (extract)
- 300 g/9 oz/2 1⁄4 cups plain (all-purpose) flour
- 2 teaspoons baking powder
- 2 teaspoons ground allspice
- 1⁄2 teaspoon cinnamon
- finely grated rind of 1 1⁄2 oranges
- 75 g/3 oz/3⁄4 cup ground almonds
- 2 tablespoons demerara sugar

Directions:

Soak the fruit in the whiskey overnight. Preheat the oven to 160°C/325°F/gas mark 3. Cream the butter and soft brown sugar together until pale, then gradually add the beaten eggs and vanilla essence. Fold in the flour, baking powder and spices. Add the fruit and whiskey, orange rind and ground almonds. Spoon into a greased and lined 20 cm (8 inch) cake tin, sprinkle with the demerara sugar and bake in the oven for 1 1⁄2 hours. Allow to cool in the tin.

YELLOW MAN

SERVES 4

Ingredients:

- 25 g/1 oz/2 tablespoons butter
- 450 g/1 lb/1 1/3 cups golden (light corn) syrup
- 225 g/8 oz/1 cup soft brown sugar
- 2 drops of rose essence (extract)
- 2 tablespoons white vinegar
- 1 teaspoon baking powder

Directions:

Coat the inside of a saucepan with the melted butter. Pour in the syrup, sugar and rose essence, then the vinegar. Bring to the boil, then reduce to a simmer. With a wooden spoon, drop a little of the mixture into cold water. If it sets in the water, stir in the baking powder. When the mixture foams, pour it into a greased baking dish and leave to cool enough to handle. Pull the toffee-like mix until it turns yellow, then leave to set and break it into small pieces with a hammer.

STOUT BERRY

SERVES 4

Ingredients:

- 1.2 litres/2 pints/5 cups Irish stout
- 2 tablespoons rolled oats
- 1 teaspoon fresh finely chopped root ginger
- 1/2 teaspoon freshly grated nutmeg
- 2 tablespoons soft brown sugar
- 1 tablespoon honey
- juice of 1/2 lemon

Directions:

Heat the stout in a saucepan and stir in the oats, ginger and nutmeg. Bring to the boil, then simmer for 20 minutes. Strain into a warm jug, stir in the sugar, honey and lemon juice and serve very hot.

IRISH COFFEE

SERVES 1

Ingredients:

- 2 tablespoons Irish whiskey
- 2 teaspoons soft brown sugar fresh strong coffee
- fresh double (heavy) cream

Directions:

Warm a coffee cup or heat-resistant glass with hot water. Pour in the whiskey, then add sugar. Pour in the coffee, leaving a 3 cm (1¼ inch) space at the top. Top up with cream poured over the back of a teaspoon.

SCAILTIN

SERVES 1

Ingredients:

- 1 teaspoon demerara sugar
- 1 extra large measure of Irish whiskey
- 1 slice of lemon
- 6 cloves
- a pinch of freshly grated nutmeg
- a pinch of ground cinnamon

Directions:

Warm a glass with very hot water, then fill two-thirds full with boiling water. Dissolve the sugar in the water, then add the whiskey. Add the lemon slice, cloves, nutmeg and cinnamon, stirring gently. Hold in the hand, savour the aroma, sip slowly. Now order another!

Don't miss out!

Visit the website below and you can sign up to receive emails whenever Paul McGregor publishes a new book. There's no charge and no obligation.

https://books2read.com/r/B-A-ZHDQ-CIVRB

BOOKS 2 READ

Connecting independent readers to independent writers.

Also by Paul McGregor

The Irish Cookbook The Ultimate Guide To Irish Classic Recipes
And Its History Food